C000005718

Four fine wines…

ALL ABOARD

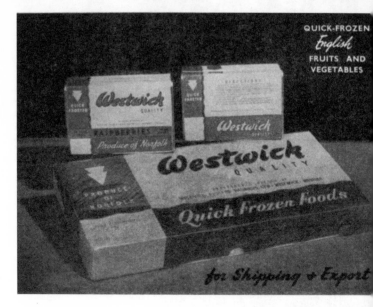

On most of Britain's fine ships—Westwick Canned and Quick Frozen Fruits and Vegetables, grown and processed in the heart of Norfolk and available from your usual suppliers.

Westwick

QUALITY

Sea Sparkle
REGISTERED TRADE MARK

QUALITY

QUICK FROZEN FISH
FOR SHIPPING

FILLETS
WHOLE FISH
SOLES
PLAICE
TURBOT
HALIBUT
LEMON SOLES
HADDOCK
MACKEREL
COD ROES
COD
SMOKED FISH
KIPPERS
AND ALL
VARIETIES

Sea Sparkle IS THE REGISTERED TRADE MARK OF ROSS GROUP LIMITED

ROSS GROUP LTD., SOUTH QUAY, GRIMSBY

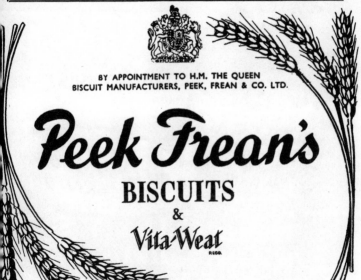

Ship Steward's Handbook

by

J. J. Trayner and E. C. Plumb

Catering Instructors,
National Sea Training School,
Gravesend, Kent

Introduction by The Rt Hon John Prescott MP

CONWAY

ACKNOWLEDGMENTS

The authors record their grateful thanks to Dr. Ronald Hope, M.A., Director of the Seafarers' Education Service and College of the Sea, for his help in the preparation of this manuscript.

Their gratitude is also due to Madame S. P. Prunier, Managing Director of the Cleveland Wine Co. Ltd., London, for reading the proofs of the chapter on wines and suggesting improvements.

CONTENTS

INTRODUCTION

A Steward at sea could work in the Cabins, Lounge or Restaurant and was known as a 'winger'.

My service was on the great Cunard Liners. For ten years, between 1955 and 1964, I sailed out of the ports of Liverpool and Southampton. We were known as the 'Hollywood Waiters' because of the smart tuxedo uniform we wore in First Class. I came from the hotel industry, where I trained as a Commis Chef. This book is an 'essential bible' for a good Steward and I do recommend it. It makes the point that a good Steward needs to know as much about food as to how good service is provided.

A Steward would spend half his working day in the Restaurant or Lounge, and as a Steward, would need to know the 'sea language' as mentioned in the excellent glossary in this book. For example, a visit to 'the Pig' meant a visit to the Crew Bar. Or up for a 'scrub out' meant washing the stairs and the decks. To do 'some dhobi' meant to wash your personal clothing – all done by 'wingers'.

The Board of Trade regulated life on board – wages, food, discipline, and so on. To challenge authority by quoting the Board of Trade Regulations dubbed you the 'barrack room lawyer', which most Officers on board believed I was!

A Steward will meet interesting people on his table – from migrants to Sir Anthony Eden. He was an ex-Tory Prime Minister who sat on my table, and prior to being Prime Minister, had been Deputy Prime Minister – a job I was to hold forty years later.

So great opportunities can come from being a Steward!

In the last ten years there has been a dramatic increase in

British shipping under the Red Ensign, particularly cruise liners and especially the return of the Cunarders. This was due to changes in legislation, of which I am proud to have played a part.

This has led to a magnificent demand for good Stewards – though under far different conditions of service than in my time. Yet it is still true that a good Steward makes a memorable voyage or cruise for the passenger, which must be their aim – and of course it is the way to a good tip!

Bon Voyage.

The Rt Hon John Prescott MP

FOREWORD

THIS handbook has been written with the needs of young ships' stewards in mind, particularly those passing through the National Sea Training Schools at Gravesend and Sharpness. It does not claim to be the last word on the subject or a complete guide to all that a steward is required to know. The aims are that these notes will guide young stewards setting out on their careers afloat, that reading SHIP STEWARD'S HANDBOOK will encourage them to read other, more detailed books, to learn all they can, and to do as well as possible in their chosen profession. We believe that actual as well as potential ships' catering personnel may learn more about the proper way of going about their daily shipboard work by studying this handbook, and that it may assist towards raising standards generally. Some may consider that we have dealt too much with table waiting in passenger liners and too little with this and other stewards' work aboard, say, tramp ships and tankers. At first glance this may appear to be a valid criticism, but on reflection it will be appreciated that although passengers and officers in cargo ships do not have large liners' arm-length menus from which to choose their meals, there is nevertheless no reason whatever why they should not be waited upon in the same competent and courteous manner as, say, first-class passengers in first-class passenger liners flying a first-class flag—the Red Ensign.

J. J. T.
E. C. P.

CHAPTER 1

PAY AND PROSPECTS

THE young man going to sea in the catering department normally undergoes nowadays a short pre-sea training course at one of the two National Sea Training Schools which were established and are operated by the Shipping Federation Ltd. One of these schools is at Gravesend, Kent, and the other at Sharpness, Gloucestershire. The annual intake at these schools is at present about 2,000 boys, who must normally be between 16 and 17 years of age. Inquiries regarding the courses should be made to: The Sea School Selection Officer, Shipping Federation Ltd., 52 Leadenhall Street, London, E.C.3. Since there is usually a waiting list, inquiries should be made some months before the boy reaches the lower age limit. Applicants must be physically fit, and the standard of eyesight should not be lower than 6/18 in each eye. A pre-sea training course is also held at the City of Liverpool Nautical Training School for ships' stewards and cooks.

After completing the course, which consists of elementary training in seamanship (e.g. lifeboat drill) and in the duties of stewards, the young steward is registered at his local M.N. Establishment office, or else proceeds to employment in a particular shipping company. An attempt is made to find employment for the steward in the type of vessel he prefers, a passenger liner, cargo liner, tramp ship or tanker, for instance.

The number of personnel in a ship's catering department and their rates of pay depend on the size and type of ship. There is nothing to stop a galley boy, pantry boy or assistant steward from climbing to the top of the ladder in his chosen profession if he is keen, ambitious and willing and able to learn.

A boy is paid from £11 12s. 6d. to £16 per month, according to the length of time he has served at sea. An assistant steward, saloon steward or messroom steward is paid £26 10s. per month. An assistant cook, assistant baker, assistant butcher, storekeeper, second cook and pantryman is paid from £27 to £28 a month, according to the job and size of the ship. A baker or butcher receives between £28 and £30 a month, a ship's cook between £32 7s. 6d. and £33 7s. 6d., according to the size of the vessel and the rating, while a chief cook will receive from £34 12s. 6d. to £36 15s. A cook-steward's rate of pay is £34 12s. 6d., a second steward's between £27 and £31, according to the size of the vessel, and a chief steward's from £36 15s. to £40 a month. A chief steward in a large passenger liner, of course, earns perhaps treble the latter figures. All the foregoing rates are with food found and are exclusive of gratuities where these are received.

On first going to sea the galley boy will spend most of his time washing dishes, scrubbing decks, peeling potatoes, etc. The pantry boy will wash up, and perhaps make tea and toast. Some passenger ships carry bell boys who act as messengers. The cleaning of galley and pantry are among the most important jobs done in a ship. People are naturally and rightly concerned that their food should be prepared in clean, hygienic surroundings, and that the food itself should be wholesome. No member of the catering department can afford to be other than scrupulously clean and fastidious both in his personal appearance and in his habits at work. Dirty utensils or waste food should never be left lying about. Everything should be stowed in its proper place and liberal use should be made of soap and hot water.

There are two ladders which the boy who goes to sea in the catering department may choose to climb. He may become an assistant (saloon, messroom, etc.) steward, who is roughly the equivalent of a commis waiter ashore. From there he may graduate to third steward and second steward. The second steward in a non-passenger ship will usually supervise service in the saloon. Above the second steward is the chief steward, who will supervise service mainly from the pantry. The chief steward may be recruited from the ranks of the second stewards or may previously have been a cook. At present there are no examinations along this road for the waiter at sea. Indeed, it is one of the few professions where a man can start at the bottom and go to the top without examination. This may not, however, be true for much longer.

Ashore, the National Council for Hotel and Catering Education (185 Piccadilly, London, W.l) has introduced a course of training for waiters, and this example may soon be followed at sea. Examinations or not, only the man who knows his job thoroughly will make the grade. A chief steward has to know how to keep records and reports, how to take inventories, how to prepare menus and order provisions, how to control men and run a most important shipboard department—in a passenger liner the catering department is far larger than the deck or engine-room departments—and much more besides. It is a great advantage to him if he speaks a second language (French in particular, but Spanish, too, is useful). Not all of these things can be learned by experience, and the ambitious steward will want to take advantage of the courses provided by the cookery schools ashore and the help which can be obtained (e.g. in English, book-keeping, French and Spanish) from the College of the Sea, Mansbridge House, 207 Balham High Road, London, S.W.17.

The galley boy or pantry boy may choose to climb a different ladder, becoming first an assistant cook, then a second cook and baker; finally, perhaps, a chief cook. In passenger vessels, of course, there are other categories of cook below the chief cook (*Chef de Cuisine*). Chief cooks, too, may become chief stewards. Here, however, he will not get far without obtaining a certificate of competency as ship's cook. Courses for this certificate are held at the following schools:

London School of Nautical Cookery—Sailors' Home, Wells Street and Dock Street, London, E.l.

City of Liverpool Seamen's Cookery School—Liverpool.

Edinburgh College of Domestic Science—5 Atholl Crescent, Edinburgh.

The Robert Gordon's Technical College—Aberdeen.

The Shipping Federation School of Nautical Cookery—Cardiff.

The Shipping Federation School of Nautical Cookery—Glasgow.

The Shipping Federation School of Nautical Cookery—Hull.

The Shipping Federation School of Nautical Cookery—South Shields.

Nautical School and School for Fishermen—Grimsby.

It is perhaps even more important for a cook to know some French than it is for a steward, since many of the best recipes come from French books and he has to be thoroughly familiar in passenger vessels with French menu terms.

Rates of pay in the Merchant Navy are now far more

attractive than ever before. Now, too, there is an Established Service Scheme whereby seafarers who choose to become "established" are assured of more regular employment than was the case in days gone by. Living conditions on board have also improved rapidly in recent years, and continue to improve. It will be seen, therefore, that employment in the catering department at sea offers prospects which compare favourably with similar employment ashore.

These notes will be of most use to the steward, particularly to the table waiter. It is here that the gap in the available literature exists, and it is this gap that the book is intended to fill. Nevertheless, all the information and advice will, it is hoped, be of some service to all in the catering department.

CHAPTER 2

PERSONAL APPEARANCE AND BEHAVIOUR

A WELL-TRAINED liner steward is a credit to himself, his ship and his company, and a good ambassador for his country. His job is to meet, to serve and to please passengers, and the manner in which he carries out these duties will greatly affect his own career and his own income. The spirit in which a job is done is quite as important as the way of doing it, and members of the catering department have a better opportunity than most other members of the crew of coming into contact with passengers, and hence of producing an atmosphere of contentment and good service. Satisfied passengers will return; courteous and attentive service, therefore, pays not only the company but the staff. The following hints are intended to assist those in the catering department of all classes of merchant ships not only to do their job efficiently but also to protect themselves.

1. Be neat, clean and tidy in appearance. Take good care of uniforms, underwear, shirts, collars, shoes, etc. Linen should always be immaculate. When cleaning and doing rough work wear a white jacket (according to the custom of the company). Wear safe footwear. Remember that passengers are most critical of the appearance of the staff.

2. Take especial care of hands and finger-nails, and be careful to clean away nicotine stains (they can be removed with pumice-stone). Do not wear jewellery, with the possible exceptions of a wrist watch and a wedding ring. The hair should be well groomed, but scent or any noticeable hair oil should be avoided.

3. Do not run, push, or indulge in any kind of horseplay. Keep hands out of pockets.

4. Be observant and constantly on the alert.

5. Do not carry bulky packages in such a way that your vision is obstructed. If travelling on deck in port while loading operations are in progress, travel on the offshore side of the

11

ship when passing open hatches. Do not carry overloaded trays; stack dishes carefully. Be especially careful when carrying glasses or sharp objects. Be careful in passing through swing doors, and keep one hand on the handrail when going up or down ladders or stairs. Watch your step when scrubbing is being done.

6. Never carry scalding liquids in open vessels. Never leave a hot-water urn or coffee urn with the steam turned on. Be careful in handling electrical apparatus, and check how many appliances can safely be used on one circuit. Draw attention to broken or defective plugs and switches.

7. Take care in placing crockery, etc., in sinks. Report broken or defective equipment. Use a pan and brush in clearing up broken crockery. Take the greatest care of all equipment. Do not deal with it wastefully or carelessly because it is not your own.

8. Clean up spilled foods and liquids immediately, and see that all foods are protected from dust and dirt.

9. Make all cutting strokes with the knife away from the body. Do not use bread-slicing machines, meat grinders, etc., unless the guards are in position.

10. Open containers properly.

11. Be careful when opening and closing ice-box doors, and when entering take the padlock inside to obviate the danger of being locked in. Learn how the alarm works, and, when working inside, look out for meat hooks. Handle cakes of ice with ice tongs.

12. Report all injuries at once, however small, and have them dressed daily until they have healed.

13. When on duty at meal times always stand at attention, and never fold your arms. Keep at a discreet distance from passengers when not actually attending them. Treat all passengers alike. Never fawn on them, but be gracious and courteous at all times. Study their preferences or "fads"— and act accordingly.

14. Do not enter into conversation with other stewards while passengers are seated in the saloon, as you might create the impression that they are being discussed.

15. Do not take part in, or appear to notice, any conversation at table or elsewhere. Do not seek conversation with passengers, but when asked for information give it in a precise, polite manner; or, if it is beyond your knowledge, refer

the matter to the chief or second steward. Do not talk about the passengers, the crew, the ship or the company's business.

16. When serving passengers, do not bring the face into close proximity with them. Turn slightly away and retain the breath as much as possible. Look after your teeth and have them regularly attended by a dentist.

17. During the service of meals carry the hand cloth over the arm and use it only for the purpose for which it is provided.

18. Think more and walk less. A little forethought may save an enormous amount of energy.

19. Co-operate to the full with other members of the staff, take your turn in the queue, and never remonstrate or criticise in public.

20. There is too much noise in the world as it is. Do not make matters worse. Go about your job quietly, always bearing in mind that a good steward is a quiet steward. There is no such being as a good noisy steward.

21. On joining a ship contact the second steward, or your leading hand, and ask his advice as to what uniform gear you will require for your particular job.

22. When you are called to turn-to, do so at once, as other people are far too busy with their own jobs to check whether you have decided to get out of your bunk or not. If you are not "on the job" when you should be, it may mean that you will be "on the bridge", and the more often you are "on the bridge" the less you will pay off with, and the smaller your prospects of re-engagement and professional advancement.

23. "First trippers" should always seek the guidance of their leading hand rather than be misled into petty misdemeanours by the so-called "sea lawyers" who appear to exist on every ship afloat, and who are always eager and ready, for some reason best known to themselves, to make disparaging remarks in an endeavour to upset the smooth running of routine duties. Needless to add, these people are usually puffed up with their own importance and keen to relate their achievements. *That they are more often than not numbered among the lower ratings, no matter how long their service at sea, is sufficient condemnation of their ability.* Being readily singled out, it is prudent to give them a "wide berth".

24. On arrival in port, permission must always be obtained before proceeding ashore. There is nothing clever or elevating in returning to the ship under the influence of drink or in an

aggressive manner. Failing to return on time for your duties not only involves breaches of discipline, but throws extra duties on maybe your shipmates, thus generating bad feeling and causing inconvenience to passengers and crew alike.

25. Lessons of the past and the combined efforts of shipping companies and unions have won you considerable improvements in your accommodation, your food and recreational facilities. Do not abuse them. Privileges are sometimes hard to gain but are easy to lose.

26. The ambitious steward is well advised not to change from company to company, but to remain in one firm's service in order to merit, according to his abilities, any promotion. Rarely, if ever, is "a trip, a ship" man found in any key position.

27. Remember, tattoos do not make you a sailor.

CHAPTER 3

CARE OF EQUIPMENT

THE main pieces of equipment used in the dining saloon
for the cleanliness of which the steward is responsible
and with the use of which he will have to be familiar are
listed below. The lists are not exhaustive and do not include
kitchen or pantry utensils and machines.

Main Types of Cutlery
Service spoon and fork: Used for serving the order from the
platter to the plate.
Soup spoon: A specially shaped spoon with a deep bowl.
Fish knife and fork: Sometimes used for hors-d'oeuvre as
well as for fish.
Large knife and fork: For main dishes which do not include
fish.
Dessert spoon and fork: For sweets. The dessert spoon alone
is used for cereals and for soups served in cups.
Fruit knife and fork: Small in size and used for fresh fruit.
Tea spoon: Used for tea, ice-cream, fruit cocktail, etc.
Spoon for grapefruit.
Coffee spoon: Smaller in size than a tea spoon.
Ice tongs: For lifting cubes of ice from the dish when used
in drinks.

Cups and Plates
Soup plate: With deep bowl.
Soup cup: With two handles.
Meat or fish plate: Large and flat.
Dessert or fruit plate: Smaller in size than for meat or fish
and slightly deeper.
Cheese plate: For bread, rolls, etc.
Salad plate: Shaped like a half-moon.
Tea plate: For bread and butter, etc. Tea services are usually
brighter and more decorative than dinner services.

15

Breakfast cup: Large.
Tea cup: Holding ¼-pint.
Coffee cup: Holding ⅛-pint.

Other Equipment

Ash trays, bread boats, casseroles (for prepared foods), cruets, cheese scoops, crumb scoops, chafing dish (lamp and stand), egg cups, entrée dishes and covers, finger bowls, flower vases, French mustard pots, fruit stands, glasses, grape scissors, ice coupes, lobster crackers, muffin dishes, nut crackers, oyster forks, pastry servers, sauce boats, serving dishes, soufflé cases, salvers, tureens (for serving soup), vegetable dishes, water jugs, asparagus tongs.

CLEANING

It will depend on the steward's particular function and the size of the ship as to how much cleaning he will have to do, but he will in any case be jointly responsible with other members of the staff for the spotless appearance of the saloon, pantry and all other parts of the ship cleaned by those in the catering department.

The golden rule. Never take it for granted that anything is clean. It is your job to make sure. *It is obvious that all gear used for cleaning purposes must, in itself, be kept clean.*

Decorative silver. Plate powder. Methylated spirits. Chamois leather. Chamois leather gloves. Camelhair brush. The powder is mixed into a paste of creamy consistency with methylated spirits; apply the paste to the silver with a soft cloth; allow to dry; take off the rough with a soft cloth; don the leather gloves; clean embossed, engraved, or filigree parts with brush, and smooth surface with chamois leather.

Table silver. Mix the plate powder into a paste with water; apply paste to silver with a soft cloth; wash silver in hot soapy, water; rinse in clear hot water; dry, and polish.

Silver dip. The silver is dipped into a container filled with boiling hot soda water, and a piece of aluminium, then rinsed in clear hot water, dried, and polished. With steel-bladed knives the silver-plated handle only is dipped. Steel blades would kill the silver dip.

Brassware. Door handles, etc., are cleaned with metal polish, which is applied to the surface with vigour. Then polish immediately. For brass port frames use brickdust, oil, and emery cloth. The brickdust is beaten into a powder; dip the emery, lightly, into the oil, then into the powdered brickdust, and apply to the metal surface. Clean, and polish with cotton waste.

Copperware. For door handles, etc.; use metal polish. For cooking utensils, use lemon, fine sand, or kitchen salt. Most cooking utensils in the galley are copper-lined. Method of cleaning: The surface is thoroughly washed to remove all foodstuff; with half a lemon, dipped in sand, or salt, apply with vigour over the complete surface. The article is then washed, dried, and polished.

Mirrors and glass table tops. Dust the surface with a linen cloth; clean with a damp chamois; polish with a linen cloth.

Polished woodwork. Since most woodwork in the saloon, and cabin furniture, is either french polished or veneered, the method of cleaning it is with a damp scouring cloth that has been rinsed in lukewarm water containing a little vinegar. Polish with a soft linen cloth.

Paintwork. Wash down with hot soapy water, rinse off with clear warm water.

Scrub-out. Bucket. Scrubbing brush. Scouring cloth. Hot soapy water. Soda. Overlap the scrub-out to prevent tide marks. With wooden decks, or tables, scrub with the grain of the timber. Change the water as often as is necessary.

Liquid detergents. These can be used for cleaning upholstery, carpets, bulkheads, deckheads; wooden, rubber, linoleum, or composition-covered desks; tables, chairs, crockery, cutlery, glass, cooking utensils; in plate-washing machines, baths, hand-basins, lavatories, etc. An additional advantage of most liquid detergents is that they are just as effective in salt water as in fresh water. As they are supplied in highly concentrated form, the chart issued by the makers should be consulted as to the quantities to be used.

See that coffee urns and similar vessels are kept clean and sweet to avoid contaminating the drinks which are brewed in them.

Glasses should be washed in warm water, rinsed in cold and dried with a linen cloth (linen does not leave fluff on the glass in the same way as cotton). If water jugs have a "waterline", clean off with potato peelings.

Silver cruets should be emptied and cleaned once a week with plate powder. Glass cruets should be washed weekly with vinegar and small lead shot, well rinsed and drained, and placed sideways on a hotplate so that they are perfectly dry before being refilled. Take special care to clean the threads of the screw. In addition to the weekly cleaning, cruets should be inspected before each service to see that they look fresh and clean. (See notes on laying the table.)

When sweeping up, use a good hair broom and sweep carefully in order to raise as little dust as possible. Sweep towards the doors, and, before sweeping the saloon, remove cloths and cutlery to the pantry. Dust all furniture. If using a vacuum cleaner on a carpet, dust bulkheads and curtains first.

Flowers need fresh water daily and should be in clean vases.

Soiled linen should be checked, taken to the linen-room, and exchanged for the same number of clean articles.

Chapter 4

LAYING THE TABLE

THE lay-ups for the officers' saloon (in which, of course, the captain takes his meals) in a cargo ship are similar to those in the officers' mess of a passenger liner, with the exception that in tramp ships and tankers the principal meal of the day, as a rule, is the luncheon, and a high tea is taken around 5 p.m. The officers' steward puts out supper, which is eaten during the night watches—tea and sandwiches, usually.

Cargo Ship Breakfast Menu
Chilled Grapefruit.
Oatmeal Porridge.   Shredded Wheat.
Fried Eggs.   Bacon.
Fresh Bread.   Marmalades.
Tea.   Coffee.

BREAKFAST LAY-UP

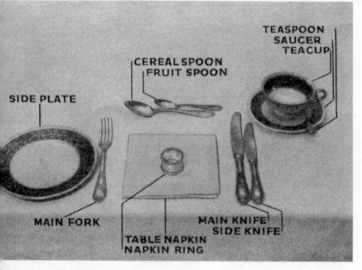

Condiments: Salt, pepper, mustard, sauces.
Centres: Milk, sugar, bread, butter, marmalades, menu card.

When compôte of fruits are on the menu it requires a dessert spoon and fork in lieu of the grapefruit spoon and the cereal spoon. If the officer wants cereals to follow, the cereal spoon is laid as the cereals are served.

When fruit juices are on the menu no fruit spoon is required because the fruit juice is served in a combination tumbler, on a side plate to the right.

When fish is the main dish, the fish knife and fork take the place of the main knife and fork.

Cargo Ship Luncheon Menu
Mulligatawny Soup.
Roast Pork, Apple Sauce.
Cauliflower. Runner Beans.
Baked and Boiled Potatoes.
Rice Milk Pudding.
Biscuits. Roquefort Cheese.
Coffee.

LUNCHEON LAY-UP

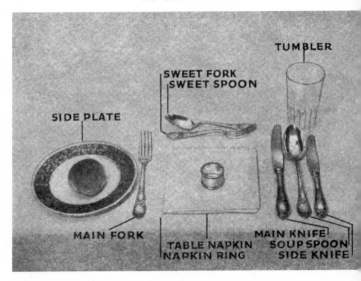

Condiments: Salt, pepper, mustard, sauces.
Centres: Sugar, butter, biscuits, cheese, iced water, rolls (on side plate) menu card.

Cargo Ship High Tea Menu
(Cold) York Ham.
Mixed Salad.
Fresh Bread.   Jams.
Tea.

HIGH TEA LAY-UP

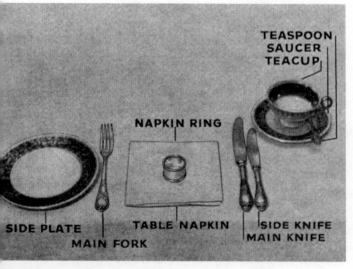

Condiments: Salt, pepper, mustard, olive oil, vinegar, sauces.
Centres: Milk, sugar, bread, butter, jams, menu card.

When fish is the main dish, the fish knife and fork take the
place of the main knife and fork.

SOME TABLE-LAYING HINTS

Study the menu carefully.

Always collect all gear required on the dumb waiter before commencing to lay up.

Dust then square off all chairs.

Unfold cloth "W" fashion on the table, and smooth with waiter's cloth, main crease of the tablecloth to run fore and aft.

Lay marker plates.

Polish all gear thoroughly before laying it on the table; polish plates and saucers individually, and do not shuffle them.

Lay cutlery, starting with main gear.

Company crest to face the passenger.

Silver to be as close as possible without actually touching, and spaced one inch from the table edge.

Balance covers with opposite covers.

Remember, finger-prints are considered to be dirt.

Lay napkins simple fold.

Tumblers upside down.

Arrange the condiments and centres attractively.

Lay the "wet centres" on the table about two minutes before the meal starts.

Check the table from the menu.

When you are satisfied the table is ready for inspection, re-polish tumblers and lay correct way up.

THE WAITER'S CLOTH

The waiter's cloth is issued before each meal to each table steward, since it is essential that the steward should commence the service with a clean one. There is generally a plentiful supply of waiters' cloths in the saloon, but the change is "one for one". A waiter's cloth must only be used for table equipment, *not* as a duster for chairs, etc. Also, the only correct way to "wear" a cloth is, over the forearm (either arm), neatly folded.

The two uses of the waiter's cloth are:

As a pad for all dishes, hot or cold, held or offered.

As a wiper for all table gear and tops and bottoms of plates etc.

Never, under any circumstances, should the waiter's cloth be carried under the armpit. That is a filthy habit. During service of a meal the waiter's cloth becomes part of his uniform, and, as such, contributes a considerable amount to his personal appearance.

THE DUMB WAITER
(The three shelf type)

The dumb waiter is often referred to as the table steward's best friend, the reason being that if it is looked after, kept clean and tidy during and after meals, it will assist greatly in carrying out his job in an efficient manner. The top shelf should be used for all glassware, clean or soiled, and the waiter's tray; the middle shelf for receiving all soiled plates and silver until the next run to the pantry; and the bottom shelf for all clean silver, napkins, fruit plates, finger bowls, etc.

Before leaving the saloon at the end of the meal the dumb waiter must be left clear and clean.

THE SERVING GEAR

Serving gear is known to a table steward as his "third hand". The spoon and fork are the most often used, but it must be remembered that there is no set routine, because according to the ability of the individual steward different foods require a different approach. A clean set of serving gear should always be used for each type of food being served.

Tourist Class

The number of passengers a steward has to serve in the Tourist Saloon is usually 16; the service, plate service. In a number of ships a second sitting is served. This means that 16 passengers are served at the first sitting, and when they have completed their meal the steward clears the table and re-lays for another 16. In all, therefore, 32 passengers are served at each meal-time. This may appear a rather formidable number, but the job is not quite so difficult as it sounds since the menu is compact. The 16 passengers being seated at the same time, it is an easy matter to ascertain how many require, say, soup. Serve this, and when clearing away the plates take the order as to how many require fish. Carry on in this fashion until the menu has been served. At the end of the first sitting, clear the table, remove all bread-crumbs, etc., re-lay the table for the second sitting, not forgetting to "trim" the condiments and centres. Sometimes when fruit is served in the Tourist Saloon the fruit knife and fork are omitted, passengers using the side knife for fruit.

Tourist Class Breakfast Menu
Chilled Fruit.
Cereals.   Rolled Oats.
Kippered Herring.
Fried Eggs and Grilled Bacon.
Fresh Bread.   Butter.   Tea.   Marmalade.

TOURIST BREAKFAST LAY-UP

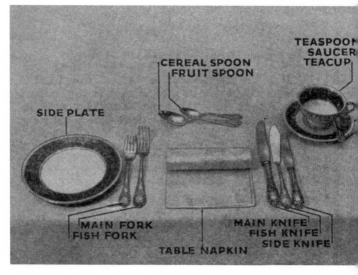

Condiments: Salt, pepper, mustard, sauces.
Centres: Milk, sugar, bread, butter, marmalade, menu card.

Tourist Class Luncheon Menu
Lentil Soup.
Spaghetti au Parmesan.
Grilled Pork Chop.
French Fried Potatoes.
Cold Buffet: Bologna.   Ribs of Beef.
Fresh Salad.
Coffee.   Bread and Butter Pudding.   Fruit.

TOURIST LUNCHEON LAY-UP

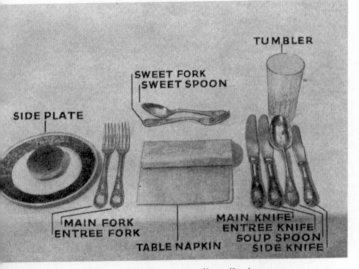

ondiments: Salt, pepper, mustard, sauces, olive oil, vinegar.
entres: Sugar, iced water, rolls (on side plate), fruit, menu card.

Tourist Class Dinner Menu
Cream of Celery.
Tronçon of Lemon Sole, Meunière.
Roast Ribs of Beef.   Yorkshire Pudding.
Rissolées and Boiled Potatoes.   Vegetable Marrow.
Apple Puffs and Custard.
Coffee.   Fruit.

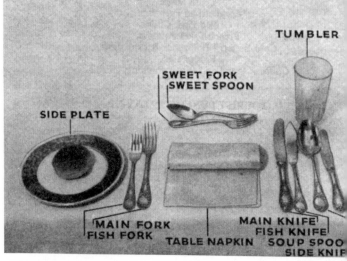

Condiments: Salt, pepper, mustard, sauces.
Centres: Sugar, iced water, rolls (on side plate), fruit, menu card.

Officers' Mess

In passenger liners senior officers invariably dine in th
main first-class saloon, each senior officer having his ow
table. The captain's table is waited upon by the captain's tige
the chief engineer's table by the chief engineer's steward, th
purser's by his steward, the surgeon's by his, and so on. A
stewards have, in addition to a table in the saloon, some oth
job to do, either as servant to one of the senior officers, or a
silver lockerman, responsible to the second steward for the ca
of all ship's silver, fruit lockerman the preparation of all frui
and fruit juices for meals and bars, the setting out of desse
baskets for dinner, etc. Other table stewards have the cleanin
of the saloon, the care of cruets, etc., to do. The junior office
may have their own mess, the stewards employed there, i
addition to waiting at table, having a set number of officer
cabins to attend to, making the beds, cleaning the cabin
valeting, and performing any cabin services required.

Breakfast Menu, Officers' Mess

Chilled Paw Paw.
All Bran.   Grape Nuts.
Puffed Wheat.   Wheat Flakes.
Rolled Oats in Milk.
Grilled Aberdeen Kippers.
Fried Lamb's Liver, Bercy.
Eggs: (To Order, 10 mins.) Fried, Turned, Poached, Boiled.
Grilled Smoked Bacon.
Fresh Bread.   Toast.
Preserves.
Tea.   Coffee

BREAKFAST LAY-UP, OFFICERS' MESS

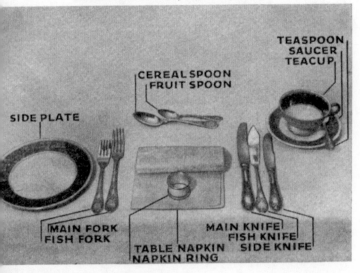

Condiments: Salt, pepper, mustard.

Centres: Castor and lump sugar, milk, butter, water jug, bread (toast is served to order), menu card.

Sideboard: Sauces, jams, honey, marmalade.

Dumb Waiter: Waiter's tray, spare silver, spare side plates, spare napkins, finger bowls, crumb scoop, serving gear, silver basket, ash trays.

Luncheon Menu, Officers' Mess
Minestrone Italienne.
Spaghetti au Beurre.
Braised Steak and Carrots.
Sauté and Purée Potatoes.
Assorted Cold Meats.
Salad in Season.
Apple and Gooseberry Pie.
Cheese.   Coffee.

LUNCHEON LAY-UP, OFFICERS' MESS

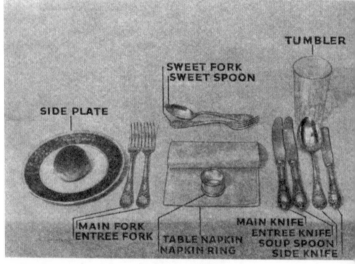

Condiments: Salt, pepper, mustard, olive oil, vinegar.

Centres: Powdered sugar, butter, rolls, water jug (containing iced water) menu card.

Sideboard: Sauces, biscuits, pickles, spare rolls, cheeses.

Dumb Waiter: Waiter's tray, coffee cups, saucers and coffee spoons spare silver, spare side plates, spare napkins, finger bowls, crumb scoop, serving gear, silver basket, ash trays.

Cream Marie-Louise.
Fillets of Hake, Meunière.
Aubergines Mexicaine.
Roast Ribs of Beef. Raifort.
Château and Boiled Potatoes.
French Beans.
Chocolate Pudding.
Cheese. Dessert Coffee.

DINNER LAY-UP, OFFICERS' MESS

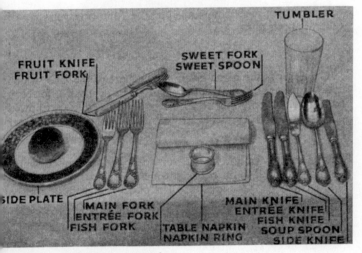

Condiments: Salt, pepper, mustard.
Centres: Powdered sugar, dessert, rolls, water jug, butter, menu card.
Sideboard: Sauces, biscuits, spare rolls, cheeses.
Dumb Waiter: Waiter's tray, coffee cups, saucers, coffee spoons, spare silver, spare side plates, spare napkins, finger bowls, crumb scoop, serving gear, silver basket, ash trays.

In the officers' saloon the menu is not so heavy as in the main saloon. Also the service differs, for in the main saloon there is the full silver service, whilst in the officers' saloon there is what is called plate service, i.e. the food is drawn from the officers' pantry on the plate and ready to serve. Stewards should remember always to wipe the bottom of the plate before placing it on the table, and to make sure the food has been placed on the plate to make the dish appear as appetising as possible. If food is placed on the plate tastefully, it helps considerably towards the enjoyment of the meal. More than three plates should never be carried at one time.

CHAPTER 5

WAITING AT TABLE

A N attractively laid table makes even simple food appear more appetising, and helps to promote good feeling among passengers. Some of the details of table-laying will vary with each company, but the following rules are of general application.

The Cover

The cover is the name given to that part of the table which is set out complete with cutlery and glass, or glasses, for each passenger. Twenty-four to 27 inches of table edge are allowed per person, and 11 inches are customary between the inner knife, and fork. These distances can, of course, be judged by eye with a little practice.

It is easy to arrange table silver if it is borne in mind that it should be placed in the order in which it is used, starting from the outside towards the plate. The cutlery set will, of course, depend on the number of dishes on the menu.

A first-class breakfast menu may consist of the following dishes, in the order given:

Fruit Juices
Fresh Fruits
Compôte of Fruits
Cereals
Fish
Main Dishes
Cold Meats and Salads
Hot Cakes with Syrups
Breads, Rolls, Scones and Toasts
Jams, Honey, Marmalades
Beverages

These may appear on a first-class breakfast menu as follows:

BREAKFAST MENU

Orange Juice.   Prune Juice.   Pineapple Juice.
Apples.   Oranges.   Grapefruit.   Pears.   Melon.
Figs in Syrup.   Apple Purée.   Compôte of Prunes.
Cream of Wheat.   Oatmeal Porridge.   Rolled Oats.   Corn Flakes.
Puffed Rice.   All-Bran.   Shredded Wheat.   Bran Flakes.   Grapenuts.
Grilled Cod.   Fried Fish Cakes.
Eggs: Fried.   Turned.   Poached.   Boiled.
Omelettes: Plain.   Cheese.   Ham.
Broiled Breakfast Bacon.   Kidney Sauté.
Cold: Boiled Ham.   Ox Tongue.
Radishes. Mustard and Cress.
Buckwheat, Griddle and Waffle Cakes.
Maple and Golden Syrup.
Breads: Sultana.   Wholewheat.   Vienna.   Hovis.   Vita-Wheat.
White and Graham Rolls.   Bran Muffins.   Currant Scones.
Jams.   Honeys.   Marmalade.
Teas: Indian.   China.   Ceylon.
Coffee.   Chocolate.   Cocoa.
Nescafé.   Ovaltine.

BREAKFAST LAY-UP

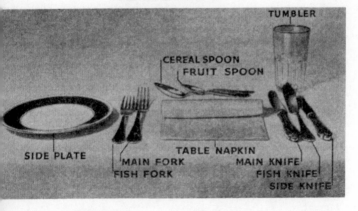

Condiments: Salt, pepper, mustard, olive oil, vinegar.

Centres: Castor and lump sugar, milk, butter, water jug, menu card. Hot rolls, scones, etc., are served when the passengers are seated.

Sideboard: Sauces, biscuits, pickles, jams, honeys, marmalades.

Dumb Waiter: Waiter's tray, breakfast cups, saucers, and teaspoons, spare silver, spare side plates, spare napkins, finger bowls, crumb scoop, serving gear, silver basket, ash trays.

Here is how the various dishes should be served:

Fruit Juices Served in a small glass, on a side plate, to the passenger's right.

Fresh Fruits Where hard fruits, e.g. apples and pears, are chosen, the fruit knife and fork are used. In the case of soft fruits, e.g. grapefruit and melon, a fruit spoon is used. Any of the following should be served with melon: Salt, lemon, and powdered sugar, or powdered ginger. Ask your passenger which he prefers. Grapefruit has been prepared overnight, but in case it has not been sweetened to the passenger's taste, proffer powdered sugar. Remember to serve a finger bowl, containing lukewarm water, and a slice of lemon to the passenger's left immediately he has finished. The finger bowl is removed when the passenger has used it. It is served again at the end of the meal, containing fresh lukewarm water and lemon.

Silver: Fruit spoon or fruit knife and fork.

Compôte of Fruit A spoon and fork.

Cereals Ask the passenger if he desires milk, cream, fruit, or powdered sugar with them. With porridge, Scots passengers usually prefer salt.

Fish There is usually a boiled, poached, or soused fish, and a fried or grilled fish.

Silver: Fish knife, fish fork.

Main Course Consists of eggs, cooked in various forms, bacon, kidney liver, sausages. Where eggs are concerned, ask the passenger how many required, how he wishes them to be prepared; if boiled, for how long; if fried, straight or turned. With bacon, fat, or lean, crisp, or otherwise.

Silver: Main knife, main fork.

Cold Meats The selection of cold meats is usually limited to perhaps two or three. Serve pickles, sauces, and salads.

Silver: Main knife, main fork.

Hot Cakes Served on a hot plate. Serve maple, or golden, syrup, or should the passenger prefer it, jam, or jelly.

Silver: Main knife, main fork.

Hot rolls, scones, etc., are served as soon as the passenger is seated.

When a passenger asks for jams, or marmalades, ascertain first the type, then the brand. For instance: Marmalade—Bitter? Orange? Lemon? Then, Robertson's? Hartley's?

Needless to say, the more courses a passenger takes, the more silver will be required. Additional silver should be added as required; this avoids overcrowding on the table.

Now proceed to lay the table for the sample breakfast menu

The tablecloth and napkins have been drawn from the linen-keeper, and laid in a convenient place in the saloon. You have a table for eight (that is the usual number of passengers where there is a full silver service), and the tablecloth has been folded in a "W" fold for easy laying. Spread the cloth on the table with the hem innermost, dust chairs, place them in correct position, polish, and place the eight side plates to the table to assist as "markers" for spacing the silver. Polish and place all knives on the right of the side plates, then polish and place all forks on the left of the side plates. Complete the silver lay-up by polishing and placing the spoons. When placing silver on the table, hold it by the base. Polish and place the eight tumblers, upside down, on the table. Remove the side plates to their correct position. With the napkins on a salver, use a serving spoon and fork to lay them in position on the table. The laundry fold is sufficient. **Once they have been handled they are considered to be soiled.** When that part of the table has been completed, the condiments and centres—milk, butter, and iced water—are placed on the table just before the meal commences.

Now to checking the table. With silver, the company's crest is uppermost; with crockery, the crest is facing the passenger. When the lay-up meets with your satisfaction, turn the tumblers upright. This is a signal to the head waiter that your table is ready for inspection. Fold the waiter's cloth neatly over the arm, and stand to attention by the table.

Stance whilst serving.—Right arm, right foot forward. Left arm, left foot forward. Point of foot between chairs; other foot at right angles.
Putting on plates.—Right arm and right foot in.
Service.—Left arm, left foot in.
Clearing plates.—Right arm, right foot in.
Waiter's cloth.—Either arm to suit individual.

Let us have an imaginary run-through serving a first-class breakfast menu.

As the passenger approaches the table, pull out a chair, and with a cheerful "Good morning" assist him to be seated. Then place the menu on the table, to his right.

PASSENGER: Orange juice, steward, please.
STEWARD: Thank you, sir.

All beverages are served to the right. When the passenger has finished the fruit juice, remove the glass, and plate, from the right, at the same time handing him the menu. Then—

STEWARD: What would you care to follow, please?
PASSENGER: Shredded Wheat, please.
STEWARD: With milk, cream, or fruit, sir?
PASSENGER: Milk, please.

When collecting the cereals, collect the hot rolls and scones from the baker's shop, serve the cereals to the passenger's left. Come round to his right, and remove the fruit spoon. Take the powdered sugar and milk from the centre of the table, and place them beside the passenger's right hand. Wait until he has used them, then replace them in the centre of the table. The unused silver return quietly to the dummy. Place the rolls, etc., in the centre of the table. The passenger has finished the cereals, so again present the menu to the right. As he considers what he will have to follow, remove the cereal plate from the left.

PASSENGER: I think I will have eggs and bacon.
STEWARD: Two eggs, sir?
PASSENGER: Yes, please.
STEWARD: Fried straight, or turned, sir?
PASSENGER: Turned, please.
STEWARD: And the bacon crisp, sir?
PASSENGER: Yes, and I would like a cup of tea, please.
STEWARD: Certainly, sir. Ceylon, Indian, or China?
PASSENGER: Indian, please.
STEWARD: With lemon, sir?
PASSENGER: No, thanks.
STEWARD: Thank you, sir.

During the conversation remove the fish knife and fork, the knife from the passenger's right, the fork from his left. Polish, and place the hot plate on the passenger's left, draw his attention to the eggs and bacon on the silver flat before transferring them from the flat to the plate with the serving spoon and fork by saying: "Your eggs and bacon, sir." His acknowledgment will be a slight inclination of the head, or some word of approval. There are two reasons for this. First, the dish must meet with his approval before it is put on the plate, and second, the chef has placed the eggs and bacon on

34

the silver flat to show them to their best advantage. Remove the eggs and bacon from the flat, again serving from the left, holding the flat close to the plate to avoid spills, taking care not to break the yolks of the eggs when transferring them from the flat to the plate. Come to the passenger's right, take the salt, pepper and mustard from the centre of the table, and place them close to the passenger's right hand.

STEWARD: Sauce, sir?
PASSENGER: Yes, H.P., please.

Carrying your tray, get a bottle of the required sauce from the main sideboard in the saloon. When serving the sauce, first shake the bottle well. Do not remove the cap or cork, and place the bottle at the passenger's right hand. Return the salt, pepper and mustard to their original position in the centre of the table. When the passenger has used the sauce, replace the stopper, then return it to the main sideboard. To prepare the tea, place the cup, saucer and teaspoon on the passenger's right. First, the sugar.

STEWARD: How many sugars, sir?
PASSENGER: One, please.

When pouring out the tea, inquire if it is strong enough. Inquire as to how much milk. When the passenger has completed the course he will place the knife and fork together in the centre of the plate. He has done that, so off we go again: the menu to the right, whilst you go to the left to clear away the breakfast plate, returning to the right to take the order.

PASSENGER: Griddle cake, please.
STEWARD: With maple, or golden syrup, sir?
PASSENGER: Maple syrup, please.

Place the hot plate and a main fork on the passenger's left, main knife on his right, transfer the griddle cake from the flat to the plate, on the passenger's left, serve the syrup jug on the passenger's right, and immediately he has used it remove it. The passenger has finished that course, therefore again present the menu to the right, remove the plate and knife and fork from the left, and place the side plate in front of him.

PASSENGER: Nothing more, steward.
STEWARD: Thank you, sir.

Remove the side plate from the left; from the right place the cup and saucer in front of the passenger. On the left, serve a finger bowl containing lukewarm water and a thin slice of lemon. Remove the finger-bowl when used. If smoking is permitted, place a clean ash tray on the passenger's right. When offering a light, use matches, not a lighter. When the passenger wishes to rise from the table, assist him by removing the chair. Then—

STEWARD: Was your breakfast to your satisfaction, sir?
PASSENGER: Yes, thank you, steward.
STEWARD: Thank you, sir.

Always endeavour to anticipate the passenger's requirements. Be courteous. Serve to the very best of your ability.

LUNCH AND DINNER

An informal lunch, or dinner, will probably consist of three or four simple courses, e.g.:

> Hors-d'oeuvres, or Soup.
> Meat or Fish course.
> Sweet.
> Biscuits and Cheese, or a Savoury.

A formal lunch, or dinner, will consist of a large variety of dishes for each of which special cutlery is required.

Course 1. This may consist of one of the following:
   (*a*) Hors-d'oeuvres. Small fork, or fish knife and fork.
   (*b*) Grapefruit. Grapefruit spoon.
   (*c*) Melon. Dessert spoon and fork, or fruit knife and fork.
   (*d*) Oysters. Small fork.
   (*e*) Smoked Salmon. Fish knife and fork.

With oysters (or clams) serve thin brown bread and butter or small crackers and lemon, tabasco, and horseradish sauce, or any other condiments provided, or desired.

Course 2. Soup. A tablespoon or specially shaped soup spoon.
Course 3. Fish. A fish knife and fork.
Course 4. Entrée. A large knife and fork.
Course 5. Roast. A large knife and fork.

Course 6. Sweet. A dessert spoon and fork.
Course 7. Savoury. A small knife and fork.
Course 8. Dessert. A fruit knife and fork.

A small knife is used throughout the meal for buttering toast, roll, or bread, and coffee will follow the dessert.

The cutlery for courses 2, 3, 4, 5 and 6 only are placed on the table for each passenger, the remaining cutlery being added just before the course is served.

In addition to the cutlery, each cover must be supplied with:

1. A table napkin, laid flat on the table. When used more than once they should be kept in a napkin ring. The napkin is placed in the middle of the cover.

2. A side plate, placed on the left of the fish fork.

3. In formal meals, a name card. Sometimes this is placed in the centre of the cover, on the side plate, or above the dessert spoon.

4. A glass, or glasses. Not more than four glasses are placed at one time on the table for each cover. They are arranged in square or diamond formation by the side of the bowl of the soup spoon, the largest glasses being placed farthest from the table's edge. At most they should include:

    (a) A Sherry glass.
    (b) A Burgundy or Claret glass.
    (c) A Champagne glass.
    (d) A tumbler for water, soft drinks, or spirits.

All are set only where all these drinks are likely to be taken. An alternative method of arranging wineglasses is to place them in a diagonal line across the top of the cutlery on the right hand of the cover. The glass for first use (sherry) should be nearest to the passenger, and so on. This is also convenient for removal by the waiter of glasses no longer required.

If port is taken, the glass is placed by the side of each passenger at the beginning of the dessert course. A liqueur glass may be placed by the side of the passenger during the dessert course, or served from a salver when requested.

After inspection by the head waiter, glasses should never be turned down on the table, and nothing should be poured into them before passengers are seated.

Table linen, cutlery, glass and silverware should all be spotlessly clean. Chipped glassware or crockery should never be used in the saloon.

Make full use of trolleys or dumb waiters where provided and see that they are always kept neat and tidy.

Cruets should be kept filled. Salt, pepper and mustard must be on the table, the number of cruets, bottles of sauce, etc., per table depending on the practice of the company. Prepared salt is drier than kitchen salt and therefore pours more easily. Salt should never be left overnight in silver salt cellars unless they have glass linings. The holes of salt and pepper pots must be kept clear; for filling, a small paper or bakelike funnel is useful. Mustard must be fresh and can be mixed with water, milk or vinegar. Fresh mustard should be served with each meal. The consistency should be such that it drops easily but not too quickly from the spoon.

Sauce bottles should look clean and fresh, and this applies especially to the stopper, which is apt to become clogged with unsightly accumulations of dried sauce.

Jam and marmalade dishes should be emptied, cleaned and refilled daily. Sugar dishes and milk jugs should always look fresh.

Table decorations, flowers, etc., if used, should be kept low so that passengers can talk easily over them. They should look fresh and the simpler they are the better.

Menu cards, if in French, should be in good French. They should not be written in a mixture of the two languages. They should be placed on the table and on no account kept on the steward's person.

Keep water jugs or bottles filled with iced water at all times.

Where cutlery and crockery bears the company's crest, the crest on cutlery should face upwards, and the crest on plates should be towards the passenger square to the table's edge.

It is customary for table stewards to stand by their tables at least 15 minutes before each meal, and to satisfy themselves that all gear is complete, clean and ready for inspection.

Stewards should assist one another. The waiter assigned to a particular table should help his passengers to their seats, but, if he is engaged, any other waiter who is free should assist in this way.

After passengers are seated, it is the waiter's first duty to provide iced water—this is of primary importance with American passengers. Fresh rolls should be on the tables at all meals; also, for lunch and dinner, nuts and iced celery and olives are usual in most companies. In the case of iced water and butter, the wishes of the passenger should be ascertained, whether he wishes to be helped to them, or just have them left within reach.

At lunch and dinner the wine waiter should present the wine list immediately. If he is otherwise engaged, the table waiter should perform this duty. Give passengers time to study the menu, but be at hand to answer inquiries should these be made.

At all meals, after passengers have been served with grapefruit, soup, hors-d'oeuvre, etc., the order for the next course should be obtained to ensure prompt service and avoid delay, this procedure to be followed after each subsequent course.

Stewards should remove from their tables any silverware not required by passengers. For example, if soup is not taken, the soup spoon should be removed, thus keeping the table neat and tidy. Cutlery, etc., must never be carried on one's person.

Do not remove condiments, preserves, etc., from a passenger's table at another station without first asking permission.

Make certain that all plates for hot meals are hot and that cold plates are really cold. The bottoms of plates, dishes, etc., should be cleaned before placing them on the table. Hot dishes must be covered.

When dishes are handed, they should, of course, be complete with the necessary serving utensils on the dish. When the steward serves he should use the fork and spoon together with one hand. Do not use the same fork and spoon for green vegetables as those used for serving potatoes. Always lift the food clear. Never let it slide from the dish on to the plate. Hold all dishes near the plates when serving as this will avoid spilling gravies, etc., on to the tablecloth and result in neater and cleaner service.

Mint sauce, bread sauce, horseradish cream, etc., should be presented in sauce boats. Apple sauce (or some other special sauce) is always served with roast duckling. Green salad may be served with roast poultry, if required. With wild duck, hare and game serve red currant or guava jelly. When serving game see that the correct garnish is provided according to the menu.

See that the passenger you are attending has everything required before serving the next.

Any item of food dropped on the floor must be disposed of and not re-served. Any item of cutlery dropped should be replaced with clean, and not used until after being thoroughly washed.

When carrying cutlery, etc., always use baskets or trays whether for laying or clearing the table, and it is desirable to place a napkin on the tray to prevent noise.

When placing plates on the table and presenting dishes to passengers, always do so from the left-hand side. Remove plates from the left hand if possible. Serve wines, water, etc. on the right of the passenger and do not fill glasses to the brim.

Fruit plates should be used only for fruit. Salad plates should be used for all salads, both green and mixed, when served with poultry, game, cold meats, etc. Mixed salads, such as Salade Russe, when included in hors-d'oeuvres, should be served in the usual manner for that course.

Finger bowls should be provided with dessert, when it is customary to serve a plate on which is placed a small decorative mat and, on top of this, a finger bowl with the dessert knife and fork lying on each side of the bowl. The finger bowl should be half filled with slightly warmed water with a thin slice of lemon or a few flower petals floating on top. The water must not be warm enough to make the finger bowl steamy.

When serving a private dinner, begin with the lady on the right of the host, and go round with each course, serving the host last.

When serving coffee, always do this by putting the *demi tasse* (half cup) and saucer on a small china plate.

Always clear and brush your table clean before serving fruit. If the tablecloth has been spotted during the meal, spread a clean napkin over it. Individual glasses which contain wine etc., should, of course, be left.

The tablecloth should, of course, be right side up, i.e. the hem should be on the underside of the cloth, and should hang evenly on the table. If it has to be changed while passengers are at table (for example, if a bottle of wine has been spilt over it) it should first be cleared and the crumbs brushed off on to a crumb tray or plate. The clean cloth should then be spread on the far side of the table from the waiter, and drawn over the table as the other is drawn off by taking hold of both cloths at once. In this way the cloth is spread without revealing the table. In no other circumstances should tablecloths be stripped while any passengers remain seated in the saloon.

When double sittings are operated, waiters must see that the condiments are properly trimmed for the second service and the tablecloth changed if necessary.

All stewards waiting at table must be thoroughly acquainted with all dishes on the menu and, where they are displayed, should pay special attention to the list of "Explanation of dishes" exhibited in the pantry. The head waiter will usually give any special instructions before each meal.

The following list offers a few reminders for particular dishes which may appear on the menu:

Apple Pie	Does the passenger like cheese with it?
Artichokes	Which kind of sauce? Melted butter, vinaigrette?
Asparagus	Mousseline, etc. Finger bowls should be provided if asparagus tongs are not available.
Baked Potato	Butter normally served. Sometimes paprika.
Caviare	(The roe of the sturgeon.) Lemon, onions, egg, butter, freshly made toast (Melba toast) may be served.
Cereals	With milk, cream, sugar, salt or fruit?
Cocoa	With whipped cream ? Served with crackers?
Coffee	Large or small? Black or with cream or hot milk? If iced, with plain or whipped cream?
Cold Game	Always supply cayenne and red currant jelly.
Cold Meats	Mustard, pickles, sauces, vegetables, salad?
Corn on the Cob	Melted butter, corn skewers?
Eggs	How many? How prepared? If boiled, how long and does the passenger want them opened? If fried, straight or turned? If "dropped," see glass is warm.
Foie Gras Fried Oysters Grilled or Fried Fish }	Crackers (toasted or plain) or toast? Which kind of sauce? Melted butter, etc.
Fruit Cocktails	Powdered sugar should be proffered.
Game	Usual accompaniments, chip or straw potatoes, bread sauce, gravy, red currant jelly, etc.
Hot Cakes Waffles French Toast }	Maple syrup, honey, jam, jelly, etc.?
Macaroni	Grated cheese, etc.?
Melon	Lemon, salt, powdered sugar, powdered ginger?
Mutton	Currant jelly?
Oysters	How served: crackers, horseradish, cocktail sauce, lemon? Provide oyster fork.
Oyster Stew	Milk, cream, or half and half? Crackers?
Poultry	White or dark meat? Gravy, bread sauce or other sauces, garnishing, etc.?
Roast Beef	Rare, medium, or well done? Thick or thin slices? Horseradish, mustard or French mustard?
Roast Lamb	Mint sauce or jelly?
Roast Pork	Apple sauce, crushed pineapple? With or without stuffing?

Salads	Which kind of dressing? Oil, vinegar, mayonnaise, etc.?
Savouries	Cayenne ? Red currant jelly?
Soups	Melba toast or crackers? Turtle soup: lemon? Bortsch: Beet juice and sour cream? Cheese and croûtons?
Spaghetti	Tomato sauce, etc.?
Steaks	Rare, medium or well done? Which kind of sauce?
Tea	With lemon, milk or cream? India or China?
Toast	Thick or thin? Light or dark? Dry or buttered?
Turkey	Cranberry sauce?
Veal	Stuffing?

A la Carte Orders

When accepting *à la Carte* orders the passenger should be told the length of time the dish or dishes will take to prepare, and when ready the waiter is responsible for seeing that the order is executed quickly and correctly.

The approximate times required for various dishes are as follows:

Beef

Chateaubriand	20 to 30 minutes.	
Filet Mignon	10 „ 15 „	
Porterhouse Steak	20 „ 40 „	
Sirloin Steak	10 „ 15 „	
Tenderloin Steak	12 „ 20 „	

Mutton

Thick Chops	25 to 30 minutes.

Lamb, etc.

Lamb Chops	10 to 15 minutes.
„ Steaks	15 „ 25 „
Veal Cutlets	10 „ 15 „
„ Chops	15 „ 20 „
Pork „	15 „ 20 „

Poultry, etc.

Roast Poussin	15 to 20 minutes.
„ Spring Chicken	30 „ 40 „
Grilled „ „	20 „
„ Poussin	15 „
Roast Squab	25 „ 35 „
Grilled „	15 „
Roast Pheasant	30 „
„ Partridge	15 „
„ Grouse	15 „
„ Quail	10 „
„ Woodcock	10 to 20 „
„ Snipe	10 „ 20 „

Note.—These times are required *after* you have given your order to the kitchen clerk.

Never lay clean linen on chairs, and see that all soiled linen goes into the linen baskets or bags kept for the purpose. Do not use table napkins for cleaning purposes, but the hand cloths or towels provided.

Make as little noise as possible when handling dishes, silverware, china, etc., using them with the greatest care, always avoiding damage to bulkheads, furniture and woodwork. Do not use tables or chairs to stand on.

When clearing away, keep the clean things separate from the used crockery, pile like things together and smaller things on top of the larger. Do not pile cups or tumblers inside one another. Collecting crockery from the table is an art which it takes practice to acquire. It is customary when collecting plates to hold one in the left hand and to carry the others in the left wrist. As each plate is collected the knife is placed on the first plate, the remains of food are carefully scraped on to the first plate with a fork and the fork is then also placed on the first plate. This leaves the plate, carried on the wrist free to receive the next, and so on, and the right hand free to collect it.

Great care must be taken in receiving passengers' orders. Nothing must be assumed or taken for granted. Trouble will be avoided by listening attentively and, if necessary, using an order pad. When you have received the full order, make sure you transmit it correctly to the kitchen. When going to the kitchen do not pass offensive remarks; it is of the utmost importance that perfect harmony exists between kitchen and saloon.

Before serving, make sure that you have all the necessary commodities which should accompany it. When a meal has been ordered for a specified time, be sure it is promptly served.

On no account should passengers' requests be refused before submitting them to the head waiter or second steward, who will in turn submit them, if necessary, to the restaurant manager, chief steward or other official. If you are in doubt about anything, do not hesitate to ask, since the best steward never knows his business too well. Success in a profession will only come to those who are willing to acquire a thorough knowledge of their job.

In the event of criticism from a passenger regarding anything served which is not to his complete satisfaction, the waiter should immediately call the attention of the head waiter or other official to the complaint, and every effort should be made to rectify the matter to the satisfaction of the passenger, even though the complaint may appear unreasonable.

Whenever a comment or complaint is made it must be reported immediately to the restaurant manager, second steward or head waiter, as it is only by reporting complaints to someone in authority that the desired results can be achieved. Further, the waiter's own responsibility is minimised when he has reported any incident to the right quarter.

Stewards should not normally accept letters or telegrams from passengers, but refer them to the purser or the inquiry office. If, however, in order not to disoblige a passenger, letters or postcards are accepted, they must be handed immediately to the official in charge of the mail office.

It frequently occurs that a passenger does not understand some of the items printed on the menu, but a steward is more likely to give offence than to receive thanks should he presume to offer advice without being asked. Should a passenger arrive in the saloon late, when perhaps the pantry service has closed down, always ask him to be seated. If at breakfast, offer him tea or coffee, rolls, butter, and marmalade. Notify the head waiter, who will then instruct you as to what to serve. Never tell a passenger: "You are too late."

When children are at the table, be guided by the parents' wishes. Place a cushion on the seat, assist the child with the napkin, and when you have time endeavour to cut the food for the child. Try to be helpful at all times.

To lay the table in rough weather, spread the cloth in the usual manner, sprinkle lightly with water, adjust the fiddles, then proceed to lay up in the normal way.

FIRST-CLASS LUNCHEON MENU

Hors-d'oeuvre	Sweet Gherkins. Sardines. Spanish Pimentos. Oeufs, Mayonnaise. Tunnyfish. Smoked Salmon. Tomatoes, Vinaigrette. Herrings-in-Tomatoes. Salade Nicoise. Ripe and Queen Olives. Saucisson: Lyon, Salami and Mortadello.
Soups	Consommé Julienne. Crème St. Germain.
Fish	Poached Cod. Parsley Sauce. (Cold): Golden Prawns. Mayonnaise.
Entrée	Spaghetti, Meat Sauce. Fried Calf's Liver and Bacon.
Joint	Shoulder of Mutton, Caper Sauce.
Vegetables	Macédoine of Vegetables. Lima Beans. Fresh Spinach.

Potatoes	Baked Jacket. Mashed.
	Saratoga and French Fried.

Grill   Spring Chicken.
(To order, 15 minutes)

Cold Buffet   Roast Ribs of Beef.   Ox Tongue.   Roast Lamb.
          Leicester Brawn.   Pressed Beef.   Boiled Ham.

Salads   Lettuce.   Tomato.   Mercedes.

Dressings   Cream.   French.   Russian.

Sweets   Rusk Pudding.   Blackcurrant Tart.
      Compôte of Peaches, Raspberries, or Rhubarb.

Ices   Vanilla.   Coffee.   Neapolitan.

Cheeses   Cheddar.   Cream.   Gorgonzola.   Camembert.
                Kraft.
             Fresh Fruit.
           Tea.   Coffee.

LUNCHEON LAY-UP

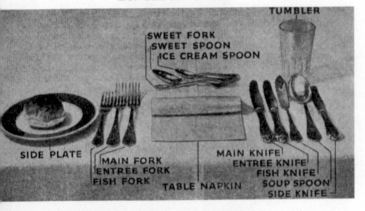

Condiments: Salt, pepper, mustard, olive oil, vinegar.

Centres: Powdered sugar, butter, rolls, water jug (containing iced water), menu card.

Sideboard: sauces, biscuits, fruit, pickles, spare rolls, cheeses (if they are not served from the trolley).

Dumb Waiter: Waiter's tray, coffee cups, saucers, and coffee spoons, spare silver, spare side plates, spare napkins, finger bowls, crumb scoop, serving gear, silver basket, ash trays.

In some companies, especially where there are two sittings, coffee and tea at luncheon and dinner are served in the public rooms, but when they are served in the saloon add lump sugar to the centres.

45

SERVING THE LUNCHEON MENU

Hors-d'oeuvre

Are served from a trolley, or a tray, each item being in individual dishes. The selection is usually around 20 dishes. Where a trolley is used, it is wheeled to the table for the passenger to make his own choice.

The most expensive hors-d'oeuvre dishes are: Caviare (prepared sturgeon roe), Paté de Foie Gras (prepared goose-liver), Smoked Salmon.

Silver to be used: Hors d'oeuvre fork.

Soups

Two thin and one thick soups are served. Thin, or clear, soups are known as consommé, or essence; thick soups as potage, crème, or purée. Consommé-en-Tasse is clear soup, served in a two-handled china cup. Consommé froid is cold consommé, and Consommé-en-Gelée, consommé in jelly form.

A selection of soups: Asparagus. Barley Broth. Cabbage. Celery. Chicken, Chicken Broth. Fish. Nettle. Oxtail. Oyster. Pea. Tomato. Turtle. Mock Turtle. Lentil. Mulligatawny. Minestrone. Mushroom.

Silver: Soup spoon.

With lentil, or pea, soup serve croûtons.

With mulligatawny, serve quarters of lemon.

With minestrone, serve grated Parmesan cheese.

Soups are drawn from the main pantry in individual silver bowls. The hot soup plate is placed before the passenger, the soup bowl is held over the plate, and gently tipped, away from the passenger.

Fish

A choice of two: one boiled or poached, the other fried, grilled or cold.

A selection of fish: Salmon. Trout. Pike. Flounder. Plaice. Halibut. Herring. Brill. Carp. Cod. Haddock. Mackerel. Perch. Sole. Red Mullet. Sturgeon. Tunny. Turbot. Eel.

Silver: Fish knife and fork.

Anchovies are used in sauces and hors-d'oeuvre; Bismarck herring in hors-d'oeuvre; sardines in hors-d'oeuvre and savouries.

Parsley sauce served with boiled fish; mustard sauce with fresh herrings; hollandaise, or mousseline, with boiled fish; mayonnaise with cold salmon.

Serve a slice of lemon with fried fish. Mango chutney, Bombay duck and grated coconut with curried fish.

Shell Fish

Lobster. Crayfish. Crawfish. Shrimps. Crab. Oysters. Mussels. Prawns. Clams.

Serve mayonnaise with Lobster, Crayfish, Crawfish, Crab, Prawns.

Oysters: Buttered brown bread, lemon and horseradish, and cocktail sauce.

Milk, cream, or tabasco with boiled oysters.

Entrée

Again a choice of two dishes.

Silver: Entrée knife and fork.

Entrée dishes: Chicken Cutlets. Lamb Cutlets. Vol-au-Vent. Ox Tongue. Sheep's Tongue. Compôte of Pigeon. Salmi of Game. Sweetbreads. Fricassée of Tripe. Calf's Head. Asparagus. Artichokes. Corn-on-the-Cob. Kromeskis à la Russe. Croquettes. Hamburgers. Vienna Steaks. Pojarke. Curried Meats. Curried Fruits. Curried Vegetables. Curried Eggs. Fricassée of Chicken.

Vol-au-Vent: Puffed pastry containing diced, or cubed, pieces of chicken, or asparagus tips.

Compôte of Pigeon: Pigeon with the addition of other game or fowl flesh.

Fricasée: White flesh served in a thick brown or white sauce.

Sweetbreads: Pancreas (glands).

Asparagus, served with butter sauce. *Silver* used: Asparagus tongs.

Artichokes, Globe Artichokes, the flower is eaten. Asparagus and Artichokes served cold, vinaigrette sauce.

Corn-on-the-Cob: Serve butter sauce. *Silver:* Corn skewers.

Kromeskis, Croquettes, Hamburgers, Pojarke, and Vienna Steaks are minced meats, prepared in various styles.

With all curried dishes serve mango chutney and Bombay duck (dried strips of the bummalo fish), grated coconut.

Main Luncheon Dishes

Boiled Beef. Boiled Mutton. Boiled Chicken. Steak and Kidney Pudding. Steak and Kidney Pie. Ox-tail. Stewed Lamb. Stewed Steak. Stewed Rabbit. Irish Stew. Cottage Pie. Sea Pie. Hot Pot.

Vegetables

A surface vegetable (e.g. cabbage), a root vegetable (e.g. carrots) and a pod vegetable (e.g. peas) are usually served.

A selection of vegetables: Peas. Beans. Cauliflower. Leeks. Onions. Kohl Rabi. Cabbage. Carrots. Celeriac. Turnips. Brussels Sprouts. Parsnips. Sauerkraut. Spinach. Tomatoes. Macédoine of Vegetables. Sea Kale. Savoys. Broccoli. Vegetable Marrow. Chicory.

Kohl Rabi: Similar to a turnip, is cooked in the same fashion.

Sauerkraut: A white cabbage.

Macédoine of Vegetables: Mixed vegetables, cubed or diced.

Broccoli: Similar to cauliflower.

Chicory: The root is cooked in the same manner as parsnips, the leaves being used in salads.

Potatoes	Baked Jacket. Boiled. Roast. Baked. Noisette: Diced small, fried. Garfield: Mashed, then dry baked. Balls: Mashed, rolled in egg and bread-crumbs, then fried. Snow: Boiled in their skins, peeled, then sieved. Creamed: Mashed with butter, and milk added. Sauté: Parboiled, diced, fried with diced fatty bacon. French fried: Chipped. Saratoga: Crisps. Fritters: Sliced thick, dipped in batter, fried in deep fat.
Grills	Are always cooked to order. The time required for cooking is plainly stated on the menu. A selection of grills: Steaks. Chops. Chicken. Game. Mixed.
Cold Buffet	Is one of the show pieces in the saloon at luncheon. The cold larder chef is in attendance to comply with the passengers' wants, from 10 to 20 meats being available. A selection for the cold buffet: Roast Meats. Roast Game. Roast Poultry. Brawns. Pies. Hams. Sausages.
Salads	Apple. Asparagus. Beetroot. Cabbage. Cucumber. Egg. Italian. Lettuce. Potato. Tomato. Endive. Raw Vegetable. Watercress. Mustard and Cress. Radishes. (For Salad Dressings, see page 56.)
Sweets	Hot and cold sweets, and ices of various flavours are served. A selection of sweets: Macaroni. Spaghetti. Vermicelli. Sago. Rice. Tapioca. Semolina. Blancmange. Fruit Salad. Fruit Pies. Fruit Jellies. Fruit Tarts. Pancakes. Compôte of Berries. Fruit Puddings.
Ices	Vanilla. Strawberry. Plain. Raspberry. Chocolate. Fruit Cocktail. Ice Cream Sundae. Coffee.
Cheeses	Strong: Gorgonzola. Limburger. Roquefort. Medium strong: Stilton. Camembert. Medium: Cheddar. Cheshire. Edam. Gruyère. Processed: Kraft. St. Ivel. Velveta.
Fruits	Apples. Pears. Peaches. Etc.

AFTERNOON TEA

Afternoon tea is served in the Public Rooms around 15.30 hours.

Afternoon Tea Menu

Brown and White Buttered Bread.   Assorted Sandwiches.
Toasted Tea Cake.   Fruit Cake.   Toast.
Sweet Biscuits.   Assorted Pastries.
Jams.   Honey.
Indian and China Teas.
Toast and Toasted Tea Cakes are served as requested.

AFTERNOON TEA LAY-UP

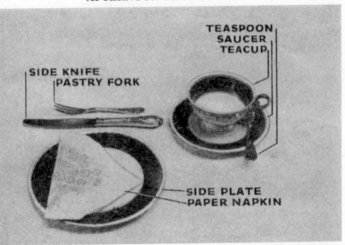

Tables Centres: Milk, lump sugar, jams, honey, plates of pastry, buttered bread, fruit cake, sandwiches, and sweet biscuits; also a small plate containing thin slices of lemon.

HIGH TEA

High tea is a meal served in circumstances such as some passengers disembarking before dinner. As the preparation of dinner for passengers who are not disembarking is at this time already under way, high tea menus are usually of dishes that require little preparation.

High Tea Menu

Poached Egg on Poached Haddock.
Assorted Cold Meats, Russian Salad.
Macédoine of Fruit and Cream.
White and Wholemeal Bread.   Tea Cakes.
Assorted Pastries.
Jams.   Honey.
Indian and China Teas.

HIGH TEA LAY-UP

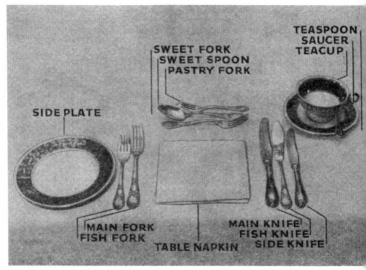

Condiments: Salt, pepper, mustard, olive oil, vinegar, sauces.
Centres: Milk, lump sugar, butter, bread, pastries, menu card.

FIRST-CLASS DINNER MENU

Hors-d'oeuvre	Hors-d'oeuvre, Variés.
Soup	Consommé Renaissance. Potage Nemours.
Fish	Darne of Salmon. Fried Whitebait.
	Hollandaise. Au Citron.
Entrée	Duckling Croquettes. Ris de Veau Pique.
	Green Peas. Forestière.
Joint	Roast Quarters of Lamb. Mint Sauce.
Vegetables	Broccoli, Polonaise. Boiled Onions. String Beans.
Potatoes	Boiled Roast. Snow. Garfield.
Grill	Escalope of Pork. Sauce Robert.

(To order, 10 *minutes)*

Assorted Cold Meats

Salads	Lettuce. Escarole. Parmentier. Tomato.
Dressings	Cream. French. Roquefort.
Sweets	Pouding Soufflé Palmre. Coupe Alexandra.
	Charlotte Russe. Patissière Française.
Ices	Pistachio. Tutti Frutti. Raspberry.

Devilled Sardines.

Dessert.

Coffee.

DINNER LAY-UP

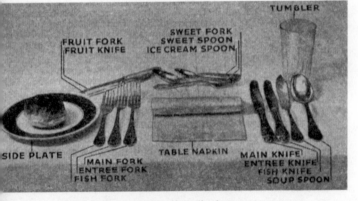

Condiments: Salt, pepper, mustard, olive oil, vinegar.

Centres: Powdered sugar, dessert, rolls, water jug, menu card.

Sideboard: Sauces, biscuits, spare rolls, pickles.

Dumb Waiter: Waiter's tray, coffee cups, saucers and coffee spoons, spare silver, spare side plates, spare napkins, finger bowls, crumb scoop, serving gear, silver basket, ash trays.

THE DINNER MENU

Hors-d'oeuvre	At dinner, the selection of hors-d'oeuvre are too numerous to mention. There are various pastes on fingers of toast, and many titbits skewered on cherry sticks. They are served sometimes in the public rooms in addition to the saloon.
Soups	As at luncheon.
Fish	As at luncheon.
Entrée	As at luncheon.
Joints	Roasts: Beef. Lamb. Mutton. Pork. Veal. Poultry. Game.
Vegetables	As at luncheon.
Potatoes	As at luncheon.
Grills	As at luncheon.
Cold Meats	The selection is usually limited to perhaps four.
Salads	As at luncheon.
Sweets	Four or five.
Ices	As at luncheon.
Savoury	A titbit to round off the meal.
Dessert	Is the show-piece of the saloon at dinner, just as the Cold Buffet is the show-piece at luncheon. In addition to a good variety of choice fruits, placed tastefully in the dessert basket, there are Nuts, Raisins, Crystallised Fruits and Gingers. Remember grape shears and nut crackers in the dessert basket.

THE MENU EXPLAINED

In some passenger liner companies it is the custom of the head waiter after he has inspected the saloon and found everything to his satisfaction to call the waiters around him instruct them to check the menu and if there is any dish on it that they do not understand explain it to them. He points out that nothing could be more embarrassing than that a passenger should ask how a particular dish on the menu is prepared, or what it is composed of, and the waiter be unable promptly to answer. Some companies print a "Definition of culinary terms" daily, and this is usually placed on the notice board in the pantry. The following is an example:

DEFINITION OF CULINARY TERMS
(L) Lunch. (D) Dinner.

Soups
(L) Consommé Nationale: Consommé garnished with Red and Green Royale.

(L) Potage Jackson: Purée of Flageolets with Julienne of Leeks. Cream.

(D) Croûte au Pot: Petite Marmite Consommé garnished with diced vegetables, and served with Croûtes.

(D) Velouté Aurore: A light Cream Tomato Soup garnished with diced Tomatoes.

(D) Cold—Consommé Madrilene: Consommé with celery flavour and Pimentos garnished with Tomato Julienne, Sorrel and Vermicelli.

(D) Cold—Crème d'Oseille: Cream of Chicken and Sorrel.

Fish
(L) Kingfish, Grenobloise: As Meunière garnished with slices of Lemon, Capers and chopped Parsley.

(D) Fillet of Sole, Marguéry: Poached and garnished with Shrimps and Mussels, coated with White Wine Sauce, glazed and served with Fleurons.

(D) Fillet of Brill, Mirabeau: Broiled and served with Anchovy, Butter, Anchovy Fillets, Olives and chopped Tarragon.

Farinaceous and Eggs
(L) Scrambled Eggs, Magenta: Garnished with diced Ham, Tomato Concassée, Chipolata Sausages on side, Tomato Sauce and Fines Herbes.

(L) Salvator Omelette: Eggs mixed with Truffle, Ham and Mushrooms in Julienne.

(L) Western Omelette: Omelette with Ham, Mushroom, Red and Green Peppers, Onions, Tomato Concassée.

Entrées
(L) Beef Goulash, Hongroise: Pieces of Beef, seasoned with Paprika, fried with Onions, dice of Tomatoes, and a little Tomato Purée, diced Potatoes.

(D) Noisette of Lamb, Navarre: Garnished with Button Onions, Tomato Concassée.

Grills
(L) Veal Chop, à la Sassi: Veal Chop, marinated in Oil and Sage, served with half Tomato.

Salads
(L) Chinoise Salad: Macédoine of Vegetables mixed with Mayonnaise, Julienne of Carrots, Truffle and Gherkins around.

(D) Snowflake Salad: Lettuce, Orange, Coconut and Pineapple.

(D) Mimosa Salad: Lettuce, Grapes, Orange and Grapefruit.

53

Sweets
  (D)   Coupe Eugénie: Marrons Glacé, Vanilla Ice Cream, Maraschino
        flavour, sprinkled with candied Violet.
  (D)   Soufflé Moscovite: Flavoured with Curaçao and Strawberry.
Savoury
  (D)   Canapé Radjah: Ham Purée with Curry, covered with Chutney.

SUGGESTED MENUS

On page 56 there is a menu—a table d'hôte menu—printed
in the ordinary way. Opposite are two suggested menus, as
they are called, one in English and one in French. If a
passenger chooses either of the suggested menus, then there is
no need to present the menu afterwards, but as he finishes each
course, serve the following one until the menu is completed.

SAUCES AND DRESSINGS

Sauces are semi-liquid foods devised to make other foods
look, smell and taste better, and hence more easily digested
and beneficial to the body.

Mayonnaise	Egg yolks, mustard, icing sugar, salt, cayenne, vinegar, olive oil.
Vinaigrette	Salt, black pepper, cayenne, parsley, paprika, vinegar, olive oil, pimento, onion, cucumber pickle, green pepper.
Tartare	Parsley, tarragon, salt, pepper, wine vinegar, shallots, gherkins; French mustard, dry white wine, mayonnaise.
French	Salt, pepper, sugar, olive oil, mustard, vinegar, a rub of garlic.
Russian	Mayonnaise, chilli sauce, Indian relish, icing sugar, horseradish, caviare.
Hollandaise	Butter, egg yolk, salt, cream, lemon juice, pepper.
Thousand Island	Mayonnaise, onion, chilli sauce, stuffed olives, green peppers, heavy cream.
Mousseline	Hollandaise sauce with equal amount of whipped cream added.
White Sauce	Flour, butter, milk, salt, pepper, squeeze of lemon juice.
Caper Sauce	White sauce, with boiled mutton liquor, and chopped capers added.
Parsley Sauce	White sauce, chopped parsley.
Onion Sauce	White sauce, chopped onions.
Cheese Sauce	White sauce, grated cheese, cayenne pepper.
Celery Sauce	White sauce, chopped celery.
Apple Sauce	Sour apples, sugar, brown gravy.

| Mint Sauce | Mint leaves, sugar, salt, pepper, boiling water, vinegar. |
| Maître d'Hôtel | Butter, lemon juice, salt, chopped parsley, pepper. |

Sauces and Savoury Jellies

Steak Cutlets	Browned butter sauce, fried onions.
Roast Mutton	Red currant jelly.
Roast Duck	Apple sauce, sage and onions.
Roast Pork	Apple sauce, roast potatoes.
Roast Lamb	Mint sauce, currant jelly.
Roast Goose	Orange sauce.
Roast Veal	Watercress sauce.
Roast Chicken	Bread sauce, grilled bacon, Saratoga potatoes
Boiled Beef	Boiled carrots, suet dumplings.
Boiled Chicken	Crème sauce.
Boiled Mutton	Caper sauce.
Boiled Rabbit	Onion sauce, grilled bacon.
Grills	Proprietary sauces: H.P., O.K., A1., etc.

A SELECTION OF GAME

Grouse. Woodcock. Blackcock. Partridge. Snipe. Ptarmigan.
Wild Duck. Guinea Fowl. Pheasant. Teal. Deer. Hare. Rabbit.

A SELECTION OF POULTRY

Turkey.   Duck.   Duckling.   Goose.   Chicken.   Spring Chicken.

MEAT COURSES—BEEF

Beefsteak	Beef Goulash	Boiled Beef	Braised Beef
Meatballs	Minced Beef	Loin of Beef	Fillet of Beef
Oxtail	Roast Beef	Rump Steak	Beef Sausages

MEAT COURSES—VEAL

Breast of Veal	Calves' Kidneys	Calves' Liver
Roast Veal	Fillet of Veal	Ribs of Veal
Sweetbreads	Veal Cutlets	Veal Stew

MEAT COURSES—MUTTON AND LAMB

Shoulder of Mutton	Mutton Cutlet (chop)	Lamb Cutlet (chop)
Irish Stew	Roast Lamb	Roast Mutton
Lamb Stew	Mutton Stew	Fillet of Mutton
Saddle of Mutton	Spring Lamb	Sheep's Kidney

MEAT COURSES—PORK

| Pork Sausages | Pigs' Trotters | Roast Pork | Bacon |
| Pork Chops | Spare Ribs | Sucking Pig | Ham |

METHODS OF PREPARATION

Salamander: to brown off	Chafing Dish	Spirit Lamp
	Boiling	Braising
Baking	Roasting	Sauté-ing
Grilling	Stewing	Deep Frying
Steaming	Smoked	Pickled
Paper Bag	Salted	

===

LUNCHEON

Hors-d'oeuvre
Tomato Juice Cocktail   Clam Juice
Green Peppers,   Vinaigrette.   Chou-fleur à la Huile.
Salade Parmentier.   Celeriac,   Julienne.   Artichauts,
Oeuf.   Anchois.   Bismarck Herrings.   Canapé de Jambon.
Saucisson: Liver, Aries and Salami.
Olives: Queen and Farci.

Soup
Bouillon Bourgeoise   Scotch Broth.

Fish
Fillet of Bass, Meunière.
Cold: Salmon, Mayonnaise.

Farinaceous
Ravioli, Italienne.

Vegetarian
Plain or Mushroom Omelettes (to order).

Entrée
Vienna Sausage and Sauerkraut.
Cervelle de Veau, Beurre Noir.

American Speciality
Turkey à la King.

Vegetables
Braised Onions.   Brussels Sprouts.
Stuffed Tomatoes.

Potatoes
Baked Idaho, Sweet, Mashed and French Fried.

Grill
(To order)
Minute Steak,   Maître d'Hôtel.
Brochette of Chicken Livers.

Cold Buffet
Roast Beef.   Ox Tongue.   Roast Lamb.   Boiled Ham.
Capon. Terrine of Duckling. Home-made Brawn.

Salads
Hearts of Lettuce.   Escarole.   Beetroot.   Tomato.
Delmonico.   Cole Slaw.   Mixed Bowl.

Dressings
Roquefort.   Thousand Island.   French.

Sweets
Rice and Apple Meringue.   Fruit Flan.
Compôte of Peaches, Raspberries or Plums.

Ices
Vanilla.   Neapolitan.   Chocolate.

Cheese
Roquefort.   Cream.   Gruyère.   Gorgonzola.
Port Salut.   Edam.   Brie.
Fresh Fruit.
Tea.   Coffee.

SUGGESTED

Hors d'oeuvre, Variés
———
Scotch Broth
———
Cold: Salmon, Mayonnaise
———
Turkey à la King
Mashed Potatoes
———
Mixed Salad Bowl
———
Fruit Flan
———
Coffee

Hors-d'oeuvre, Varies
———
Bouillon Bourgeoise
———
Bass de Mer, Meunière
———
Entrecôte à la Minute
Pommes Frites
———
Salade Escarole
———
Compôte de Fruits
———
Fromage   Café

MENUS

CHAPTER 6

WINES

EVERY steward should know how to serve wine. It is als
interesting and useful to know something about it. The
is a lot to learn which cannot be summarised in a fe
pages. The expert, like André Simon, spends a lifetime
acquiring this knowledge. Mr. Simon has written a great ma
books on the subject and so have many other people. Most
these books can be borrowed from the College of the Sea if yo
want to know something of the theory as well as the practice
drinking wine! Once they have been bottled, most win
improve for a time, but eventually they begin to grow flat a
bitter and may turn vinegary, the great wines doing this on
after many decades.

The following outline is only a guide to the use of wines a
much depends on personal taste. In general, however, tho
who can afford to drink different wines with their meals beg
with lighter wines and finish with heavier and stronger wine
Most people, too, prefer a sweet white wine with a sweet di
at the end of a meal, or with the fish at the beginning, and dri
red wines or champagne with meat courses.

Wines served before Meals (Aperitifs)

The French word *apéritif* means something which sharpe
the appetite. Such wines should not be sweet and should
sipped. Most people are content with just one glass if oth
wines are to follow. Aperitifs may be served before meals or
the beginning of a meal with the soup or hors-d'oeuvre. The
can be divided into three main classes:—

(i) **Dry Sherries.** Sherry is a wine of golden colour whi
is made from white grapes. It is a blend of wines, whi
accounts for the infinite number of varieties. Sherry com
from southern Spain, and nowadays some of the South Afric
and Australian wines which resemble sherry are very goo
The label on the bottle should tell you the name of the fir

responsible for the blending of the sherry and it may also describe the *type* of sherry by using one of the following words: (a) *Fino,* which should mean that the wine is very dry and pale in colour, and of the highest quality. (b) *Manzanilla,* which should mean that the wine is even drier and paler than *Fino,* and has a salty taste to it which some people prefer. (c) *Amontillado.* This is perhaps the most popular. It has an attractive "nutty" bouquet of fragrance, and is not so pale or dry as the other two.

(ii) **Vermouth.** The best vermouths come from France and Italy, but they can be made from any white wine, since the particular flavour comes from the wormwood, herbs, spices and other things). French vermouth is drier and lighter in colour than Italian and the best-known brand is that sold under the name of *Noilly-Prat.* Owing to the addition of burnt sugar in its preparation, Italian vermouth is darker and sweeter, Martini Rossi being the best-known in this country.

(iii) **Commercial Brands.** There are many commercial brands of aperitif. Most of them are served neat and chilled in a wineglass, but sometimes they are served with water (or gin and iced). Some of the better-known French brands are: Amer Picon, Byrrh, Dubonnet, Pernod and St. Raphael.

Wines served during Meals

Wines served during meals are either red, white or pink in colour. Generally speaking, white wines are made from white grapes and red wines from black grapes, although some white wines come from black grapes if the skins are removed before they have time to colour the wine. Champagne, for example, is made from black and white grapes. Pink wines are not in themselves very notable and the famous Blancoe Blancs is made only from white grapes, but they are becoming more popular, especially Tavel from the Rhône Valley, pink champagne, and the excellent *Natural* Pinot Rose wine — Sancerre; the best wines are normally either red or white. Where you do come across pink wines they are best served chilled, like white wines, and usually taken at lunch with fish or white meats.

(i) **Red Wines.** The standard for all red wines served with meals is set either by the French wines from the Bordeaux district (claret) or by the French wines known as burgundy.

Burgundy is stronger and deeper in colour. Nowadays some very good red wines come from other parts of the world, but the best French wines from the best vineyards are still the most sought after and the most expensive.

The best wines from the Bordeaux district are never blended and are known by the *Château*, *Clos*, *Cru* or *Domaine* (that is the vineyard) where the grapes are grown. It is also essential to know the year in which the grapes were harvested before deciding if it is likely to be a good wine. The finest clarets come from the Médoc area, and some very good ones from the Graves district (though most people associate this name with white wines), but again it must be emphasised that only by knowing the vineyard and the vintage year can the best wines be chosen. Claret should be served at room temperature.

The Burgundy wine region is really three separate districts. The best red burgundies come from the Côte d'Or (Golden Slope). The *best-known* red burgundies are those of Beaune and Pommard, while most people, too, are familiar with the name *Beaujolais*. Unfortunately, since these names are easy to remember they have been very much abused, and the only means of knowing the best is to become familiar with the names of particular vineyards and the reputable shippers. Burgundy should be served 5 deg. cooler than clarets.

Chianti is the best-known red wine of Italy and is bottled in flasks. It is suitable for oily and highly spiced foods, but has not the body and charm of the best French wines. Some Algerian red wine is good and cheap, and red wines also come from South Africa, Australia, the United States and many other places.

(ii) **White Wines.** White wines are clear yellow or amber in colour but may become deeper in colour as they are matured. Most white wines are somewhat sweet to the taste, but Moselle, Rhine (hock), Alsace, Chablis and Graves wines are drier than Sauternes and the wines from Anjou and the Palatinate.

Chablis, from the Burgundy wine region, is perhaps the best known of the white wines, and if genuine is the palest amber in colour with an almost greenish tinge to it. Moselle wines are light and delicate, and with more bouquet than body. Hock have more colour and are stronger. Graves sometimes smells of sulphur and should be cheaper than those already mentioned. The sweetest of all white wines are the Sauternes, which are made just south of Bordeaux, and the best of these is the wine known as Château Yquem of a good vintage year.

Champagne, the grapes for which are grown mostly in the valley of the River Marne, is a pale white wine in a class on its own and is usually drunk mostly on special occasions. It can be drunk from the beginning and right through a meal and the bottle is served from a bucket of ice. Champagne must not be over-iced—only slightly so.

There are other sparkling wines, burgundies, hocks and Moselles, but they are more popular in America than in Great Britain.

Wines served at the end of Meals

Wines served at the end of meals are called "fortified" or dessert wines, and the most popular are port, sherry, Madeira and Marsala. All these have been "fortified" or strengthened by the addition of brandy in their preparation.

There are many different types and qualities of port, the best coming from the upper valley of the Douro River in Portugal. The wine is offered for sale under a variety of names. Vintage port, like any other vintage wine, is the product of the grapes of a particular year. Ruby port is usually a blend of different vintages, while tawny port can be either similar wine aged for many years in casks or else a blend of ruby and white port. Neither tawny port nor ruby port has the body and bouquet of the vintage wines. All are made from black grapes. There is also a white port, which is amber in colour, always sweet, and sometimes very sweet.

After-dinner and dessert sherries are darker and sweeter than those served as aperitifs. The finest are the Oloroso and Amoroso types, but old brown sherries are not now so widely drunk as they were.

Madeira is made and matured in the island of that name. The best guarantee is the name of a well-established shipper, and it is a rich wine usually known by the name of the type of grape (e.g. Malmsey) from which it is made. Madeira, being a white wine, can be enjoyed after champagne.

Marsala is the best fortified wine which comes out of Italy, more like madeira than sherry. In colour it is a beautiful dark amber; in taste it is more sweet than strong. The *Florio* company is one of the reliable sources of Marsala, which is useful for various sauces and sweets as well as for drinking.

Spirits and Liqueurs

Liqueurs are taken with coffee after the dessert. Among the better-known liqueurs are cognac (brandy), Cointreau and Grand Marnier (both made from orange and cognac), also "La Trappistine" (Old Armagnac) brandy base, Chartreuse and Benedictine (both originally made in the famous French monasteries after which they are named), curaçao (manufactured mainly in Holland from a variety of orange grown in the Dutch West Indies), kirsch (from the German word for cherries from which it is made), kümmel (with a strong flavour of caraway seed, which is one of the herbs from which it is made), crème de menthe (a rich, green liqueur made from mint and cognac), and anisette (which takes its name from aniseed, one of the principal ingredients which gives it its unmistakable aroma). There are also many fruit liqueurs including apricot and peach brandies.

Keeping and Serving Wines

Ideally, wines should be stored in a dark, dry and well-ventilated storeroom as free as possible from vibration and draught, at a temperature of about 55 deg. F. The shelves should be away from heating pipes and the bottles should be kept on their sides.

Wine bottles should be handled with care and not shaken. When serving wine, wipe the bottle clean and show it with the label exposed to the passenger. Then remove the head of the metal cap or the wax protecting the outside face of the cork neatly, wipe the upper lip of the bottle all round with a clean cloth, and drive your corkscrew slowly right through the centre of the cork and draw the cork steadily. After drawing the cork wipe the inside of the neck with a clean cloth, take hold of the bottle firmly just below the neck in the right hand (unless it is the practice of the company to use a cradle) and slowly pour its contents into the glass. Serve all drinks on the right of the passenger and always be careful not to fill glasses right up to the brim, but only two-thirds to one-half. In serving wines it is customary to pour a little into the host's glass first, let him taste it and, if he approves, serve all the other guests (the principal guest first and then others in rotation) before filling the host's glass. Do not serve any more wine from a bottle once you see some loose sediment come to the neck.

Remove empty bottles as considered advisable, and before

serving champagne see that all other wineglasses are cleared from the table. Do not on any account, when clearing glasses, put your fingers in the glasses. Do not open beer bottles, mineral waters, etc., near the tables, as passengers' clothes may be spoiled if the contents bubbles over. Similarly, champagne bottles need opening with great care.

Red wines should be served at room temperature. On no account must red wine be artificially warmed. White wines should be drunk cold, and they are often served (and champagne is always served) in an ice bucket.

When serving drinks already poured out, glasses should be presented on a salver, and empty glasses when removed should be taken away on a tray or salver. Similarly, when presenting wine bills or returning change, etc., always use a salver.

All wines or mineral waters left by passengers, which they wish to be kept for them, should be securely corked and marked on the labels with the number of the seat and passenger's name. The bottles should then be returned to the barkeeper. All stewards, when serving wine, should always see that the proper glasses are in place, and should carry at all times a well-sharpened pencil, corkscrew and crown opener, and see that the wine list is kept at hand.

Wineglasses

It is, of course, impracticable to describe all the types of glasses used in the service of drinks, and this is something which can only be learned by experience in a particular ship. In general, however, four types of glass are used. The 2½-ounce tulip-shaped wineglass is used for aperitifs and dessert wines. A 4-ounce glass is used for dinner wines, 2½- to 8-ounce glass for other drinks, and a champagne glass—which is usually saucer-shaped—is used for sparkling wines. Liqueurs are usually served in 1-ounce liqueur glasses, except for very fine brandy, which is served in very large 18-ounce glasses. All glassware should be brilliant in appearance, and the cloth used to wipe and polish glasses should never be used for anything else.

Order of Service

The order in which wines are served varies with individual tastes and pockets and the food served, but the following order is most common:

With Hors-d'oeuvres, etc.: Sherry, vermouth, and vermouth cocktails.

With Soups: Sherry, or white table wines. Madeira.

With Fish, or Shellfish: White or pink table wines, or champagne.

With Poultry: White or pink table wines, or champagne.

With Game, or Red Meats: Red table wines.

With Sweets: Sauternes, or very fine hock.

With Cheese: Red table wines, or dessert wines (vintage port, brown sherry).

With Dessert and Fruit: Dessert wines.

With Coffee: Spirits or liqueurs, cognac, Armagnac.

Serving a Bottle of Champagne

Here is an imaginary run-through the process of serving a bottle of champagne at dinner, which, of course, was ordered at luncheon, and assuming the main course is just being served

WINE WAITER: May I serve the champagne, sir?

PASSENGER: Yes, please, steward.

The waiter then removes all glasses from the table, with the exception of the champagne glasses. He then goes to the bar and asks for the wine, carefully places it on his salver, and returns to his dumb waiter, where he carefully gives the bottle a polish over. He then approaches the right side of the host (the person who has ordered the wine) and shows him the bottle allowing him to see the label, and the sealed cork.

PASSENGER: Yes, steward, that is the wine I ordered.

WINE WAITER: Thank you, sir.

The waiter then stands back a little, and proceeds to open the wine by untwisting the safety wire that secures the cork. Then, very gently, he eases the cork by giving it a slight turn keeping his cloth ready for the moment he allows the cork to pop out, in case the wine is very lively. Having removed the cork, he wipes the inside of the neck of the bottle with his cloth. Pour a little (taster) into the host's glass, stand back, and await his verdict.

PASSENGER: Thank you, steward, that is fine.

The waiter then serves the principal guest, seated on the host's right, first, continuing around the table and serving the host last. The bottle is then placed in an ice bucket, containing chopped ice, and placed in a convenient position to the host. The wine waiter then carries on with the remainder of his station, and in between serving other passengers keeps glasses topped up until wine is finished.

A LIST OF WINES, SPIRITS AND LIQUEURS

Advocaat	A Dutch liqueur, thick, and yellow in colour, made from eggs and brandy.
Algerian Wines	White, and red, not considered of very good quality.
Anjou Wines	White, French, still, and sparkling.
Apricot Brandy	A liqueur. Tawny in colour, and usually sweet.
Armagnac	Brandy (French).
Barbera	An Italian red wine, both sweet and dry.
Barolo	An Italian red wine.
Barolino	An Italian red wine.
Berncastel	A white Moselle wine.
Benedictine	The greatest of all liqueurs. D.O.M., the well-known initials, are *Deo Optimo Maximo* (To God the best and the greatest). Dating from 1510, made by the Benedictine monks.
Bordeaux	Red wines (clarets). White wines (Graves, Sauternes, Barsac).
	Clarets: **Leognan, Martillac, Pessac.**
	White Wines: **Barsac, Bommes, Fargues, Preignac.**
Bourbon	A rye whisky.
Brandy	A liqueur made from wine, brandy that comes from the Cognac district of France is known as **Cognac**.
Burgundy	Red and white wines.
	Red Burgundies: **Beaujolais, Beaune, Corton.**
	White Burgundies: **Chablis, Meursault, Pouilly.**
Calvados	Apple brandy.
Capri	An Italian red or white wine.
Champagne	The most famous of all sparkling wines, made within the limits of the former province of Champagne.
Chartreuse	A liqueur, both green and yellow.
Cherry Brandy	Made from cherries and brandy (sweet liqueur).
Chianti	An Italian red wine.
Cointreau	A form of white curaçao, made from orange and spirits.
Crème de Menthe	A liqueur, peppermint flavour, green in colour, hence the nickname, **"Starboard Light."**
Crème de Caçao	A liqueur, chocolate in colour, cocoa flavour.
Crème de Café, or Moka	Liqueur, coffee flavour.
Crème de Cassis	Liqueur, blackcurrant flavour.
Crème de Framboise	Liqueur, raspberry flavour.

Curaçao	An orange brandy liqueur.
Drambuie	Whisky liqueur.
Falerno	Red and white Italian wine.
Frascati	Italian white wine.
Gin	A spirit, distilled from barley, and rye, or from rectified molasses spirit, flavoured with juniper.
Grand Marnier	A form of curaçao, pale brown in colour.
Hock	German red or white wines.
Hollands	A spirit distilled in Holland, flavoured with juniper known as Hollands gin.
Juleps	A mixture of brandy, gin, etc., flavoured with herbs.
Kirchwasser	A white cherry spirit—serve in iced glass.
Kümmel	A clear coloured liqueur, flavour of caraway.
La Trappistine	A yellow liqueur—French. It is compounded on a base of very fine old Armagnac from an ancient recipe of the monks of the Abbaye de la Grace de Dieu France. Similar to Benedictine and Yellow Chartreuse.
Lachrymae Christi	("Tears of Christ"). A white Italian sweet wine.
Maraschino	A cherry liqueur.
Marsala	A Sicilian wine.
Moscato	An Italian sweet fortified wine.
Moselle	Wines from the vineyards of the banks of the River Moselle, both still and sparkling.
Peach Brandy	Peaches, with a brandy base.
Perry	A West Country drink, made from pears.
Port	From Portugal.
Raspail	A French liqueur.
Rufino	Italian red wine.
Rum	Spirit distilled from sugar cane.
Saumur	White sparkling from Maine-et-Loire, in France.
Sherry	A wine from the Jerez district in Spain.
Sloe Gin	A liqueur made from a mixture of gin and sloe juice.
Strega	A liqueur from Benevento in Italy.
Tokay	A golden Hungarian wine.
Vermouth	An aromatic wine, and is most popularly used in mixed drinks. French vermouth is dry, Italian is sweet. It is produced from fortified white wine with aromatic herbs blended into it.
Vodka	Russian, distilled from maize, potatoes and rye.
Whisky	Scotch, distilled from malted barley.
Whiskey	Irish, fine barley, distilled water.

MINERAL WATERS

Vichy Water   } Are natural waters which, because of their mineral
Perrier Water   } content, are said to be beneficial.
Apollinaris

Soda Water   } Are artificially aerated waters, with fruit juices
Ginger AleLemonade } added.
Ginger Beer
Grapefruit, etc.

Tonic Water   Contains quassia, which is of medicinal value against
the tropical disease of malaria.

WINE CUPS

These are long drinks, soda water being very important. Use only wine spirits such as brandy for flavouring, also good quality liqueurs, sound fruit, and plenty of ice.

Red wine cups may be sweetened. White wine cups should not be.

Example:
Claret Cup
     1 bottle claret.
     1 glass curaçao.
     2 glasses brandy.
     2 bottles soda water.
     Tablespoon lemon juice.
     Chipped ice.

WINE TERMS

Sec	Dry.
Acerbe	Made of unripe grapes.
Dry	No sweetening added.
Fortified	Strengthened with spirits.
Fameux	Heady. (In France the term is normally Capiteux).
Light	Natural, unfortified, little alcoholic content.
Vinosity	Strength of wine.
Frapper	To place on ice.
Vintage	Annual gathering of grapes.
Bottle	One-sixth gallon.
Magnum	Two bottles.

COCKTAILS

The cocktail shaker is not always used, as the followin examples will show.

Champagne Cocktail.	Dash of brandy. 3 dashes of Angostura bitters. 1 lump of sugar. Ice. Fill with champagne.
Between the Sheets.	1/3 rum. 1/3 brandy. 1/3 Cointreau. Dash of lemon juice. Shake.
Pick Me Up.	1/3 brandy. 1/3 Italian vermouth. 1/3 absinthe. Stir.

CIGARETTES, CIGARS AND TOBACCO

Tobacco should be stored in a warm place (temperature 6 deg. F.) in an atmosphere which is neither too dry nor to damp. The main types are Virginian (used in the more popul brands of cigarette), Turkish, Egyptian and Rhodesian. It part of a steward's duty to provide a clean ash tray at the rig time, and a light if required. If a passenger asks for a light, th steward should strike the match away from the passenger, a then hold the flame to the cigarette. Never use a lighter. For cigar, he should hand the passenger the box of matches.

Special knowledge of cigars, like that of wines, is on slowly acquired. The best cigars come from the Vuelta Aba district in Cuba, but good cigars are also made in Havan Jamaica, India, Burma, Manila, Mexico and Great Brita (from imported tobaccos). The leading ones are made different sizes and shapes to suit individual tastes, and may mild, strong or very strong. A good cigar produces a firm, gre ash which lasts a considerable time before falling. Nev crackle a cigar against the ear; although this indicates wheth it is dry, it may break the outside leaf which holds the cig together.

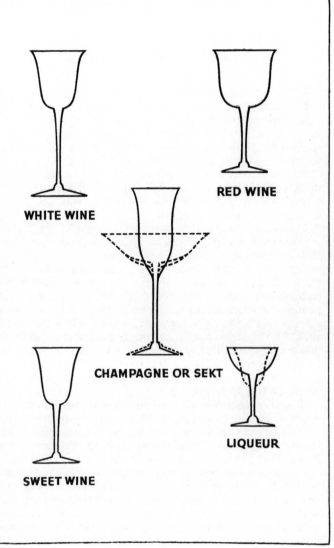

WHITE WINE

RED WINE

CHAMPAGNE OR SEKT

SWEET WINE

LIQUEUR

CHAPTER 7

BEDROOM STEWARDS

THE bedroom steward (B.R.) must have all the qualities required in the other branches of the catering department, plus the capacity to condense a day's work into four or five hours, in order that his section of cabins is ready for captain's inspection at 1100 hours daily. He must be thorough at his work, and be able to work at speed. Co-operation between B.R.s and stewardesses is essential. It is team-work that counts. The B.R.'s principal duties consist of Cabin Service, Valeting, Bedmaking, and the general cleaning of a section of cabins.

On sailing day, before passengers embark, the bedroom steward makes a final check on his cabins, sees that thermos and water bottles contain fresh, iced water, rechecks or water glasses, soap, toilet paper, ash trays, matches, bath mats, huck and bath towels, mirrors, wash-basins, coathangers and soiled linen bags. He checks bell lights, heaters, fans, and deckhead, berth and wardrobe lights, door catches and hooks, wardrobe and locker catches. Any defect should be reported to the second steward immediately. Port glasses must be checked, both inside and out, as passengers on entering a room for the first time, often walk towards the port to have a look out. Matches must not be put in rooms where children are berthed.

When the ship is in port, all ports should be closed and the doors of all unoccupied cabins locked to prevent pilferage.

Bedroom stewards must keep themselves informed as to the "Daily Programme," meal times, hours for Bureau, Baggage Room, Rail Traffic Office, Surgeon, Shops, and Libraries.

Passengers are always appreciative of personal service rendered. If any passenger requests any service out of the ordinary routine, the chief steward should be informed, and he will then give the necessary instructions and make arrangements accordingly. The bedroom steward is frequently "closer" to the passenger than any other member of the catering department, and he should therefore be particularly careful to express his willingness to be of service.

The bedroom steward should contact his passengers as soon as possible after their arrival on board, address them by name (to avoid mistakes in names the Berthing List should be checked and the Addition and Deletion Lists), introduce himself, welcome them cheerfully to their rooms, ascertain if baggage is correct, point out to each passenger where the lifebelt is stowed, and direct them to where the ship's notices are displayed concerning FIRE and Boat Stations.

Parcels, mail and flowers for passengers should be placed in rooms immediately they arrive, and a receipt obtained.

Passengers' wishes should be ascertained as to unpacking, time of morning call, and requirements when called, clothes to be pressed, time bath is required. In the case of rooms without baths, advise the bathroom steward, or stewardess, to contact the passenger. Advise passengers as regards the shoe cleaning service, available, and that shoes for cleaning should be placed outside cabins before retiring at night. Passengers should be familiarised with reservation of dining-room seating and deck chairs. A list of children's names must be given to the head stewardess, together with any particulars of special diets.

Toilets should be flushed out with clean water immediately on leaving the dock, and toilet pans thoroughly cleaned of stains caused by the dirty water in the dock.

The most important part of the day for B.R.s is from "tick-on" until "rounds" are completed, and will be spent serving early morning tea trays to his passengers when he calls them, preparing baths, clearing tea trays, and strapping-up the crockery used. Unnecessary noise in service pantries and bedroom alleyways, particularly during early morning work, must be avoided. It is not necessary for both the B.R. and the stewardess to serve morning tea to married couples. One or the other should perform this service, unless requested otherwise by the passengers. Whilst passengers are bathing, dress clothes should be put in wardrobe, day clothes brushed, and laid out ready, subject to the passenger's wishes, of course. When serving meals in cabins, dining-room service should be followed as closely as possible. Passengers are usually indisposed when they take their meals in rooms, therefore extreme tact and patience should be exercised when serving them. Aboard some liners, when a B.R. is not actually serving meals in cabins, he assists with the press service during meals.

Make all beds before tackling jobs that make the hands dirty. Soiled bed linen, towels, etc., should be changed at the usual times appointed for this purpose, but should the necessity arise, linen may be changed at any time. B.R.s should make sure there is a good supply of clean bath and hand towels in each cabin; bath mats should be draped over the side of the bath when not in use.

In bedmaking, neatness is essential. The middle crease of the bottom sheet must be in the centre of the mattress. This also applies to the top sheet, the blankets, counterpane and pillows, for it ensures an even "tuck-in" around the sides of the mattress. The company's crest on the counterpane should be central, and the "fold-back" at the top of the bed should be the depth of the pillows. When all beds have been made, dust overheads, polish mirrors, furniture and brightwork, with a clean damp cloth, sponge the carpet over, roll it up, pull the luggage and the luggage racks from underneath the beds, dust it, scrub under the beds, replace the luggage and the racks, scrub the deck and replace the carpet. Clean the bathroom in a similar manner, paying particular attention to the scuppers. Remove all soiled linen, replace with clean, clean and refill all water bottles, polish all tumblers, and check on toilet soap and paper.

When the cleaning and tidying of cabins have been completed, the pantry service locker and alleyways should be attended to; then in a clean white jacket, make a final check-up and stand by for rounds. A clean white jacket must be worn at all times when on duty. If it is taken off for the purpose of cleaning, then close the pantry doors, or if in a cabin draw the door curtains. Have all lights on and doors hooked back for daily inspection, but switch off as many lights as possible when not required: among other things, this helps to keep the ship cooler in tropical waters.

After morning inspection, when passengers are absent from their cabins, look in to see if the cabins are still tidy and, if necessary, tidy up. Remember, always knock on doors before entering. Never throw away anything that is not in the waste-paper basket, except empty boxes (such boxes should be carefully examined to see that no article of any value has accidentally fallen in). Never remove flowers from a room without the passenger's consent. Always see that there is a good supply of laundry lists in the rooms, and let passengers know when their laundry can be accepted. Also, as passengers may wish to have drinks in their cabins, a supply of wine chits should be in each room, and a wine list kept in each pantry.

The afternoon period is usually worked on a rota system, which allows one B.R. to cover several sections whilst the other B.R.s have a rest period. There is little to be done as a rule—chiefly walking round the sections QUIETLY and answering any calls that are made. Clattering of crockery or loud talking in the pantry are prohibited as passengers may be resting. Smoking, singing and whistling in passenger accommodation are forbidden at all times.

Delay in having bells answered is most irritating to passengers and should be avoided at all costs. It is desirable, though not essential, for the bedroom steward, or stewardess, attached to a particular section to answer bell calls from it. Bells must be answered immediately by any member of the bedroom staff in the vicinity, and if passengers then ask for their own steward, or stewardess, they can be informed. The main point is to get bells answered quickly and not cause delay in walking along alleyways calling the name of a bedroom steward or stewardess of section; this is disturbing to other passengers as well as, of course, annoying to passengers who are waiting for the bells to be answered since they may only require some small service which can be rendered by any bedroom steward or stewardess other than those attached to their section.

The evening period of duty, commencing between 1630 and 1700 hours, is devoted to day-to-day systematic cleaning jobs which time does not permit being done in the morning— cleaning ports, deckheads, washing paintwork, overheads, pantries, service lockers, for example. Whilst passengers are at dinner, shoes that require cleaning should be placed outside the room. Brush and place in the wardrobe clothes that have been worn during the day, turn beds back, lay out night attire and dressing gowns, place slippers by the side of the bed, fill thermos and water bottles with fresh iced water, replenish supply of soap, towels and matches as required, draw port curtains, secure all movable objects, clean baths and toilets, check toiler paper containers, and generally tidy the rooms.

When passengers return from dinner make sure they have everything they require; inquire as to what time they wish to be called in the morning, and if tea, coffee, biscuits, etc., are required; check all ports, let the night steward know which are open and put the bell-board switch on the night position.

When passengers are on board in port, ports they may wish leaving open should be covered with ratguards. Should passengers wish to go ashore for the evening, inquire as to what time they will return so that you will be on hand to open their cabins. Or, if they should be late, pass the message on to the night steward.

As soon as passengers vacate a cabin immediately prior to disembarking, make a thorough search of the room, open drawers, wardrobes and look under beds. Should anything of value be found, try to contact the passenger before he or she leaves the ship or the pier. If you are unable to contact the passenger, any article found must be handed to the chief steward or purser immediately.

In port, ascertain as to where, and at what times, rubbish is collected. When in the terminal port, strip all bed linen and with towels, curtains, etc., prepare for dispatch to the ship's laundry. Wash all paintwork in cabins, clean out all drawers, polish all furniture and brightwork, wash out all water bottles, scrub decks, switch off all lights, close all ports, and lock all cabin doors before going off duty.

When unlocking storerooms always return the padlock on to the hasp after opening the door and lock it. This prevents padlocks from being lost. Return all keys to the keyboard after use.

When told to make a "single change" it means that the top pillowcase and the bottom sheet are to be removed from the bed. The bottom pillowcase then goes on the top pillow, the clean pillowcase does on the bottom pillow, and what was the top sheet goes on the bed first, the clean sheet being placed on top.

To clean baths, and hand basins, use hot soapy water, which can also be used for cleaning chromium-plated bath fittings; polish with a soft cloth.

Shoes. When collecting shoes from cabins, mark the cabin number on the sole of the shoe with chalk.

Remove the laces from shoes before cleaning.

Remove all dirt from the shoe before applying polish.

Golf shoes, ski boots. Glycerine saddle soap, and a sponge.

Apply saddle soap to damp sponge, rub into the leather until the latter is pliable.

Black shoes. Apply the polish lightly over the complete surface, including the instep and the welt of the shoe. Polish well with first brush, finish off with polishing brush and a piece of velvet. Replace the laces.

The same applies to brown shoes.

To remove sea-water stains from brown shoes, lightly apply methylated spirits to the stained parts only, then apply saddle soap, and polish. Methylated spirits will shrink the leather. The immediate application of saddle soap prevents this.

Palm Beach shoes. Blanco the buckskin first, allow to dry, rub lightly with a fine wire brush, then polish the brown or black strappings. When the shoes are made of glacé kid instead of buckskin, clean the kid leather as with dress shoes.

Dress shoes. Lightly smear with Vaseline, polish with a linen cloth.

Suede shoes. Because of the wide variety of shades, most passengers supply their own cleaners. The method of cleaning suede is as with buckskin.

Clothing. There are very few stains that cannot be removed by using hot soapy water. To remove grease stains, place a thick piece of brown paper under the stain, a piece over the stain, and apply a hot flat iron. The brown paper will absorb the grease. Wash with hot soapy water when grease has been removed.

Dress clothes. These must be brushed with a piece of the material from which the suit is made. With full evening dress the spare piece of material for this purpose is usually found in the tail pocket. With dinner suits it is in the hip pocket.

Officers' blue uniforms. Pour a little stale coffee into a deep-bowled plate. Dip the clothes brush, lightly, into the coffee. Brush the uniform with the damp brush. Be careful of decorations since the coffee would stain them.

SOME SHIPBOARD TERMS

Aft end	Tourist section of ship.
Alleyway	Passage, or corridor.
Articles	Terms of agreement between shipmaster and crew.
Article No.	Number given to each member of crew.
Athwartship	From port to starboard, or reverse.
Bibby Alleyway	A cul-de-sac.
Blues	Navy blue uniforms.
Boss	Chief steward.
B.R.	Bedroom steward.
Bulkheads	Walls.
Commis	Apprentice waiter.
Companion way	Staircase.
Cover	A complete set of table cutlery.
Deadlight	Metalcover over port-hole.
Deck	Floor.
Deckhead	Ceiling.
Dhobi	Washing clothes.
Ducer	Second steward.
For'ard	Front of ship.
Fiddle	Ledge around the edge of the table which is raised in rough weather to prevent articles falling off the table.
Leading Hand	Petty officer.
Lockerman	Steward in charge of lockers, e.g. cruet locker, silver locker, fruit locker, etc.
Maindeckman	Steward in charge of second Steward's gear.
M.O.T.	Ministry of Transport.
Overheads	Ledges, beams, etc., above the head.
Peak (also **Glory Hole**)	Stewards' accommodation.
Pig and Whistle	Crew Bar.
Port Side	Left side of ship facing forward.
Returns	Repeat food orders. A second helping of any dish.
Rosie	Refuse bin.
Rounds	Captain's inspection.
Running Sitting	Continuous service of a meal.
Scupper	Drains.
Scuttle	Port-hole.
Scrub-out	Scrubbing floors, etc.
Show	Waiter's table section.
Side Doors	Doors in ship's side. Used when passengers are embarking, or disembarking; also for taking aboard of stores, baggage, etc.

Silver	Table cutlery, etc.
Slops	Ready-made clothing, shoes, etc., sold to the crew.
Side-job	Working routine between meals.
Sub	An allowance from pay.
Sugi	Hot soapy water.
Strap-up	Washing silver, etc.
Single Change	Changing one sheet and one pillowcase on a bunk.
Starboard	Right side of ship facing forward.
Topside	First class.
Tiger	Captain's personal servant.
Tick on	Reporting for duty.
Whites	White tropical uniforms.
Winger	Waiter.

FRENCH GLOSSARY

Abatis. *Giblets and winglets of a bird.*

Abats. *Offal, liver, heart, head, feet and tail of an animal.*

Abricot. *Apricot.*

Agaric. *An edible mushroom.*

Agneau. *Lamb.*

Agnés Sorel. *A cream chicken soup.*

Aiglefin. *Haddock.*

A la. *In the style of.*

A la Carte. *Foods prepared to order.*

Albert. *A butter sauce.*

Albion. *A chicken consommé*

Alexandra. *A chicken consommé.*

Aloyau. *Sirloin of beef.*

Amande. *Almond.*

Ananas. *Pineapple.*

Anchois. *Anchovy.*

Anguille. *Eel.*

Animelles. *Lamb's fry.*

Artichaut. *Artichoke.*

Asperges. *Asparagus.*

Aubergine. *Eggplant.*

Balzac. *A veal consommé.*

Bar. *Bass.*

Baraquine. *A veal consommé.*

Barbeau. *Barbel.*

Barbue. *Brill.*

Bar de Mer. *Sea bass.*

Bécasse. *Woodcock.*

Beignets. *Fritters.*

Beignets de Fromage. *Cheese fritters.*

Betterave. *Beetroot.*

Beurre. *Butter.*

Beurre Fondu. *Melted butter.*

Bifteck. *Beefsteak.*

Biscuit Glacé. *Icecream wafer.*

Blanchaille. *Whitebait.*

Blanquette. *A veal, or poultry, stew.*

Blonde de Veau. *Veal stew.*

Boeuf. *Beef.*

Bonne Femme. *A leek and sorrel soup.*

Bonvalet. *A cream of turnip soup.*

Bouilli. *A meat and vegetable soup.*

Brioche. *A breakfast roll.*

Brocoli. *Broccoli.*

Brochet. *Pike.*

Cabillaud. *Cod.*

Café. *Coffee.*

Café au Lait. *Coffee with (hot) milk.*

Café Noir. *Black coffee.*

Caille. *Quail.*

Canard. *Duck.*

Canard Sauvage. *Wild duck.*

Caneton. *Duckling.*

Canneberge. *Cranberry.*

Carrelet. *Flounder.*

Caviar. *Caviare.*

Céleri. *Celery.*

Cerise. *Cherry.*

Cervelles. *Brains.*

Chair à Saucisse. *Sausage meat.*

Champignons. *Mushrooms.*

Chapon. *Capon.*

Chou. *Cabbage.*

Chou de Salade. *Cabbage salad.*

Chou de Bruxelles. *Brussels sprouts.*

Chou de Mer. *Sea kale.*

Chou-fleur. *Cauliflower.*

Chou-rave. *Kohl rabi.*

Chou Rouge. *Red cabbage.*

Civit. *A brown game stew.*

Clovisse. *Clam.*

Cochon-de-Lait. *Sucking pig.*
Concombre. *Cucumber.*
Consommé. *A clear soup.*
Coq de Bruyère. *Blackcock.*
Coques. *Cockles.*
Coquilles St. Jacques. *Scallops.*
Cornichon. *Gherkin.*
Côtelettes. *Cutlets.*
Côtes de Boeuf. *Ribs of beef.*
Courgeon. *Vegetable marrow.*
Crabe. *Crab.*
Crème. *Cream.*
Crème de Riz. *Rice soup.*
Crème d'Orge. *Barley soup.*
Crêpes. *Pancakes.*
Cresson de Fontaine. *Watercress.*
Crevette. *Shrimps.*
Croissants. *Breakfast rolls.*
Croûte. *A slice of toasted or fried bread.*
Croûte-au-pot. *A beef broth.*
Croûtons. *Cubes of fried bread for serving with soup.*

Darne. *A middle cut of fish.*
Demi-tasse. *A small cup.*
Dent-de-lion. *Dandelion.*
Diablé. *Devilled.*
Dinde. *Turkey.*

Eau. *Water.*
Echalote. *Shallot.*
Eclair. *Finger-shaped confection.*
Eclanche. *Shoulder of mutton.*
Ecossaise, à l'. *Scottish style.*
Ecrevisse. *Crayfish.*
Egyptienne. *Egyptian style.*
En Croûte. *Encased in crust, or paste.*
Endive. *Salad leaves of the chicory.*
En Papillote. *Paper-bag cookery.*
En Tasse. *Served in individual cups.*
Entrecôte. *Middle cut of sirloin steak.*
Entrée. *The course following the fish.*
Entremets. *Second course dishes, vegetables, sweet, and savoury.*
Epaule de Veau. *Shoulder of veal.*
Eperlan. *Smelt.*
Epice. *Spice.*
Epinard. *Spinach.*
Epis de Mais. *Corn on the cob.*

Escargots. *Snails.*
Escalope. *Thin slices of meat.*
Esturgeon. *Sturgeon.*

Fagot. *Faggot of parsley and thyme.*
Faisan. *Pheasant.*
Fanchonnettes. *Small puff pastries.*
Farine. *Flour.*
Faséole. *Kidney bean.*
Faubonne. *Purée of haricot beans.*
Fausse. *Mock.*
Fécule de Marante. *Arrowroot.*
Fécule de Marron. *Chestnut flour.*
Fécule de Pommes de Terre. *Potato flour.*
Fécule de Riz. *Rice flour.*
Feuillage. *Leaves.*
Feuillé. *Decorated with leaves.*
Feuilletage. *Flaky pastry.*
Féves. *Beans.*
Féves d'Espagne. *Runner beans.*
Féves de Marais. *Broad beans.*
Figue. *Fig.*
Filet de Boeuf. *Fillet of beef.*
Filet de Veau. *Fillet of veal.*
Filet Mignon. *Small fillet of beef.*
Flageolet. *Green kidney bean.*
Flan. *Tart.*
Flanchet. *Flank.*
Flet. *Flounder.*
Flétan. *Halibut.*
Foie. *Liver.*
Foie de Veau. *Calves' liver.*
Foie-gras. *Goose liver.*
Fond Blanc. *White stock.*
Fond Brun. *Brown stock.*
Fondu. *Melted.*
Fondue. *Toasted, or melted, cheese.*
Fouetté. *Whipped.*
Foulque Morelle. *Coot.*
Fraise. *Strawberry.*
Framboise. *Raspberry.*
Friandines. *Savoury patties.*
Friandises. *Small confections.*
Fricandeau. *Veal brawn.*
Fricassée. *A brown or white stew of rabbit, poultry or veal.*
Frit. *Fried.*
Froid. *Cold.*
Fromage. *Cheese.*

Fromage de Cochon. *Hogshead cheese, or brawn.*
Fromage de Porc. *Pork cheese or brawn.*
Fumé. *Smoked.*
Fumet de Poisson. *Fish stock.*

Galette. *A breakfast roll.*
Gardon. *Roach.*
Garni. *Garnished.*
Gâteau. *Decorated cake.*
Gâteau à la Crème. *Layer cake.*
Gâteau aux Pêches. *Peach pie.*
Gâteau de Riz. *Rice pudding.*
Gaufre. *Waffle.*
Gelée. *Jelly.*
Gervais. *A French cream cheese.*
Gibelotte. *A rabbit stew.*
Gibier. *Game.*
Gigot d'Agneau. *Leg of lamb.*
Glacé. *Ice.*
Glacé à la Ananas. *Pineapple ice cream.*
Goujon. *Gudgeon.*
Gratin, au. *Dishes covered with grated cheese, or bread-crumbs.*
Grenade. *Pomegranate.*
Grenouille. *Frog.*
Grianneau. *Young grouse.*
Groseille. *Gooseberry.*
Gruau d'Avoine. *Oatmeal.*
Gruyère. *A Swiss cheese.*

Haché. *Minced.*
Hashis. *Hash.*
Hanche. *Haunch.*
Hareng. *Herring.*
Hareng Fumé. *Kipper.*
Hareng Marine. *Roll mops.*
Hareng Salé. *Salted herring.*
Hareng Saur. *Red herring.*
Haricot. *A mutton stew.*
Haricot Verts. *French beans.*
Homard. *Lobster.*
Hors-d'oeuvres. *Appetisers.*
Huile. *Oil.*
Huile d'Olive. *Olive oil.*
Huître. *Oyster.*
Huîtres en Cheval. *Angels on horseback.*

Hûre de Sanglier. *Boar's head.*

Jambon. *Ham.*
Jarret. *Knuckle.*
Jarret de Boeuf. *Shin of beef.*
Jeune Agneau. *Spring lamb.*
Jus. *Gravy.*

Kari. *Curry.*

Lait. *Milk.*
Laitance. *Soft roe of the male fish.*
Laitue. *Lettuce.*
Lamproie. *Lamprey.*
Langouste. *Crawfish.*
Langue. *Tongue.*
Lapin. *Rabbit.*
Lard Fumé. *Smoked bacon.*
Légumes. *Vegetables.*
Levraut. *Young hare.*
Lièvre. *Hare.*
Limande. *Lemon sole.*
Limonade. *Lemonade.*
Loche. *Loach.*
Longe. *Loin.*
Loup de Mer. *Catfish.*
Lucine. *Clam.*

Macédoine. *Diced or cubed fruit or vegetables.*
Macéré. *Soused.*
Macreuse. *Widgeon.*
Mais. *Maize.*
Mandarine. *Tangerine.*
Mangue. *Mango.*
Mansard. *Woodpigeon.*
Maquereau. *Mackerel.*
Marchpane. *Marzipan.*
Mariné. *Pickled.*
Marrons. *Chestnuts.*
Maté. *Tea made from a species of holly.*
Melettes. *Sprats.*
Menthe. *Mint.*
Méringue. *A Soufflé confection.*
Merlan. *Whiting.*
Merluche. *Haddock.*
Miel. *Honey.*
Mignardises. *Small confections.*
Mirabelle. *A small yellow plum.*

Mode, à la. *After the style of.*
Morue Salée. *Salted cod.*
Mou. *Lights.*
Moule. *Mussel.*
Moutarde. *Mustard.*
Mouton. *Mutton.*
Mufle de Boeuf. *Ox cheek.*
Muge. *Grey mullet.*
Mûre. *Mulberry.*
Mûre de Ronce. *Blackberry.*
Myrtille. *Bilberry.*

Navet. *Turnip.*
Néctarine. *Smooth-skinned peach.*
Noix. *Walnut.*
Noix de Brésil. *Brazil nut.*
Noix de Veau. *Best part of a leg of veal.*
Nouilles. *Noodles.*

Oeufs. *Eggs.*
Oeufs à la Coque. *Boiled eggs.*
Oeufs brouillés. *Scrambled eggs.*
Oeufs de Poisson. *Hard roes.*
Oeufs au Jambon. *Ham and eggs.*
Oeufs Farcis. *Stuffed eggs.*
Oeufs pochés sur toast. *Poached eggs on toast.*
Oeufs sur le Plat. *Fried eggs.*
Oie. *Goose.*
Oignon. *Onion.*
Oignons Marinés. *Pickled onions.*
Ombre. *Grayling.*
Omelette. *Omelet.*
Omelette au Jambon. *Ham omelet.*
Orge. *Barley.*

Pailles au Parmesan. *Cheese straws.*
Pain. *Bread.*
Pamplemousse. *Grapefruit.*
Panais. *Parsnip.*
Pastéque. *Water melon.*
Pâte. *Paste.*
Pâté. *Pie.*
Pâte d'Anchois. *Anchovy paste.*
Pâté de Bifteck. *Beefsteak pie.*
Pêche. *Peach.*
Perdrix. *Partridge.*
Persil. *Parsley.*
Petits Fours. *Small confections.*

Pétoncle. *Scallops.*
Pied. *Foot.*
Pieds de Veau. *Calf's foot.*
Pigeonneau. *Squab.*
Pintade. *Guinea fowl.*
Points d'Asperges. *Young tips of asparagus.*
Poire. *Pear.*
Poireau. *Leek.*
Pois. *Peas.*
Poisson. *Fish.*
Poisson Rouge. *Char.*
Poitrine. *Breast.*
Poitrine d'Oie Fumée. *Smoked goose breast.*
Poivre. *Pepper.*
Pomme. *Apple.*
Pomme de Terre. *Potato.*
Porc. *Pork.*
Potage. *A thick soup.*
Potage Parmentier. *Potato soup.*
Pot-au-feu. *A meat and vegetable soup.*
Potiron. *Pumpkin.*
Pot-pourri. *Stewed meats highly seasoned.*
Pou de Mer. *Whelk.*
Pouding. *Pudding.*
Poule. *Fowl.*
Poulet de Grain. *Spring chicken.*
Purée. *Cooked foods reduced to a pulp, or a thick soup.*
Purée de Pommes de Terre. *Mashed potatoes.*

Quartier d'Agneau. *Quarter of lamb.*
Quartier de Derrière. *Hind-quarter.*
Quartier de Devant. *Fore-quarter.*
Queue. *Tail.*
Queue de Boeuf. *Oxtail.*

Ragoût. *A meat and vegetable stew.*
Ragoût de Mouton (Irlandais). *Irish stew.*
Raie. *Skate.*
Raifort. *Horseradish.*
Reine Claude. *Greengage.*
Rhubarbe. *Rhubarb.*
Ris d'Agneau. *Lamb's fry.*
Riz. *Rice.*

Rognon. *Kidney.*
Romaine. *Cos lettuce.*
Rôti. *Roast.*
Rouget. *Red mullet.*
Roulade. *Meat balls.*
Roux. *Equal quantities of flour and fat used as the basic medium for thickening sauces.*
Russe, à la. *Russian style.*

Sagou. *Sago.*
St. Germain. *A cream pea soup.*
Salade. *Salad.*
Salade aux Oeufs. *Egg salad.*
Salade de Fruits. *Fruit salad.*
Sarcelle. *Teal.*
Saucisse. *Sausage.*
Saumon. *Salmon.*
Savoureux. *Savoury.*
Sel. *Salt.*
Selle de Mouton. *Saddle of mutton.*
Semoule. *Semolina.*
Serviette. *Table napkin.*
Sirop. *Syrup.*

Soupe. *Soup.*
Soupe au Céleri. *Celery soup.*
Sperling. *Smelt.*
Sucre. *Sugar.*

Table d'Hôte. *Fixed menu.*
Tasse. *Cup.*
Tête de Veau. *Calf's head.*
Tête de Laitue. *Head of lettuce.*
Thé. *Tea.*
Thon. *Tunnyfish.*
Topinambour. *Jerusalem artichokes.*
Tortue. *Turtle.*
Tortue Claire. *Clear turtle soup.*
Tortue Fausse. *Mock turtle soup.*
Tôt-fait. *Flapjack.*
Tournedos. *Small fillet steaks.*
Tourte. *Tart.*

Vandoise. *Dace.*
Veau. *Veal.*
Venaison. *Venison.*
Vinaigre. *Vinegar.*
Volaille. *Poultry.*

EXTRACTS FROM MINISTRY OF TRANSPORT NOTICES

Upkeep of Crew Accommodation

Regulation 34 (1) of the Merchant Shipping (Crew Accommodation) Regulations, 1953, provides that:

"The crew accommodation in every ship shall be maintained in a clean and habitable condition, and all equipment and installations required by these Regulations shall be maintained in good working order. Every part of the crew accommodation (not being a storeroom) shall be kept free of stores and other property not belonging to or provided for the use of persons for whom that part of the accommodation is appropriated, and in particular no cargo shall be kept in any part of the crew accommodation."

Crew accommodation

includes sleeping rooms, mess rooms, sanitary accommodation, hospital accommodation, recreation accommodation, storerooms and catering accommodation provided for the use of seamen and apprentices, not being accommodation which is also used or provided for the use of passengers. It should be noted that passageways serving crew accommodation are regarded as forming part of crew accommodation and are subject to the Regulations.

Inspections

Regulation 34 (2) requires that:

"The Master of the ship or an officer appointed by him for the purpose shall inspect every part of the crew accommodation at intervals, not exceeding seven days, and shall be accompanied on the inspection by one or more members of the crew. The

Master of the ship shall cause to be entered in the ship's official log book a record of:

(a) the time and date of the inspection;

(b) the names and ranks of the persons making the inspection;

(c) particulars of any respects in which the crew accommodation or any part thereof was found by any of the persons making the inspection not to comply with these Regulations."

Complaints

Regulation 35 (f) provides that:

"The crew accommodation in every ship to which these Regulations apply shall be inspected by a surveyor of ships whenever a complaint has been lodged with a surveyor of ships or with a superintendent, and complies with the following requirements:

(i) the complaint shall be in writing, signed by one member of the crew in the case of a ship of under 1,000 tons, and by three members of the crew in the case of any other ship;

(ii) the complaint shall specify the respects in which it is alleged that the crew accommodation in the ship does not comply with these Regulations;

(iii) the complaint shall be lodged without undue delay;

(iv) the complaint shall be lodged at least 24 hours before the ship is due to sail, unless the ship is in port for less than 24 hours."

Masters, officers and seamen will no doubt appreciate that the maintenance of crew accommodation in a satisfactory condition requires the full-co-operation of all members of the crew. Where applicable, the Regulations include requirements for the provision of suitable washing and sanitary facilities and for the storage of working clothes, and the crew should be encouraged to make the fullest use of what is provided. *The need for personal hygiene as well as the cleanliness of quarters is imperative and preventive action against dirt is far easier and more desirable than cure.*

Masters are also reminded that frequent and thorough inspection will tend to reduce the number of complaints.

Inspection of Food and Water

The attention of Masters is drawn to a National Maritime Board Agreement, made in connexion with the Food and Catering Convention, 1946, ratified by Her Majesty's Government.

The Agreement, which came into force on January 1, 1954, applies to every ship which is required to carry a Certificated Cook in accordance with Section 27 of the Merchant Shipping Act, 1906, which means, in effect, all foreign-going ships of 1,000 gross tons and over, which go to sea from any port within Home Trade limits.

The Master of every ship, or an officer specially deputed for the purpose by him, together with a responsible member of the Catering Department is required, not less than once per week during the currency of Articles, to inspect the supplies of food and water provided for the crew and enter the result of such inspection in the official log.

First published circa 1955

This edition first published by kind permission of the author's
estate, Mrs J. Plumb, in 2007 in Great Britain by
Conway
an imprint of Anova Books Company Limited
10 Southcombe Street
London W14 0RA

ISBN: 9781844860562

A CIP catalogue record for his book is available from the
British Library.

10 9 8 7 6 5 4 3 2 1

Printed and bound by MPG Books Ltd. Cornwall

To receive regular email updates on forthcoming Conway
titles, email conway@anovabooks.com with Conway Update
in the subject field.

www.anovabooks.com

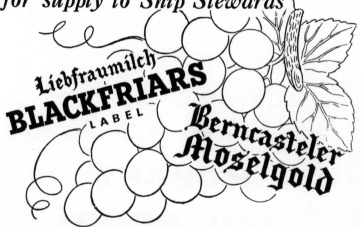

Passengers (and crew) not only like Drambuie but they usually know of the link between Drambuie and Bonnie Prince Charlie whose personal recipe was the origin of this delectable liqueur. Throughout the world Drambuie is a favourite with those who appreciate a liqueur of subtlety and distinction.

Drambuie

The Drambuie Liqueur Co., Ltd., York Place, Edinburgh.